IMAGES
of America

VANDENBERG AIR FORCE BASE

On the Cover: Pictured here on April 13, 1959, Thor/Agena launch vehicle No. 170 is being readied on Launch Pad 75-3-4 (later designated as SLC-1W). The mission was a Corona prototype and did not carry a camera. Capsule recovery failed, and due to a timing error, the capsule landed on Spitsbergen Island, Norway. The capsule was never found, though the search for it formed the basis for the book and film *Ice Station Zebra*. (US Air Force.)

IMAGES of America
VANDENBERG AIR FORCE BASE

Joseph T. Page II

ARCADIA
PUBLISHING

Copyright © 2014 by Joseph T. Page II
ISBN 978-1-4671-3209-1

Published by Arcadia Publishing
Charleston, South Carolina

Printed in the United States of America

Library of Congress Control Number: 2014930446

For all general information, please contact Arcadia Publishing:
Telephone 843-853-2070
Fax 843-853-0044
E-mail sales@arcadiapublishing.com
For customer service and orders:
Toll-Free 1-888-313-2665

Visit us on the Internet at www.arcadiapublishing.com

To Michael Keith Hardesty (1977–2012).
No stronger warrior, no greater friend, no better man could be found.

Contents

Acknowledgments		6
Introduction		7
1.	The Ranchero Era and Camp Cooke (1542–1958)	11
2.	Early Days of the Cold War (1959–1976)	29
3.	Eyes in the Sky	47
4.	Dawn of a New Era (1977–1989)	65
5.	Business as Usual (1990–Present)	83
6.	Archaeology of the Cold War	101
7.	Vandenberg Space and Missile Heritage Center at SLC-10	113
Bibliography		125
Index		126
About the Vandenberg Space and Missile Heritage Center		127

ACKNOWLEDGMENTS

This book would not have been possible without the help of one man. He goes by many aliases: The Museum Guy, JP, and Mr. Sidetrak'n. Donald "Jay" Prichard has been the soul of Vandenberg's history for decades. He has been the keeper of the flame, taking the stories of thousands of Vandenberg's occupants and distilling them into context (and humor) for generations to learn from. As a story keeper, his wisdom stretches into decades before his time as Minuteman maintenance non-commissioned officer and "Pad Daddy" at SLC-10. Props to him and puppy treats to his loyal companion, Sage.

Additional thanks to Chris Ryan and Esther Kenner from the Cultural Resources section of the 30th Civil Engineering Squadron, who knew where all the good stories and photos around base were buried. (Literally!) Special mention goes to fellow Gravelhauler Capt. Douglas Carmean for his insatiable love of missile history and pithy social media posts.

Special thanks to my editor Alyssa Jones and all the other professionals at Arcadia Publishing. They helped bring this amazing history to print.

I would also like to thank Lt. Col. Joseph Iungerman, Maj. Joseph Callaro, Lt. John P. Maggs, Jon Haeber, Jim Widlar, Wayne McMurry, Kade McMurry, Col. Charlie Simpson (Association of Air Force Missileers), and Col. David Arnold for their assistance. The help provided by the staff of the Vandenberg Library (Christine McLaughlin, Dianne Welch, and Joseph L. Carlson) was essential to the book's completion. Additional thanks to Ms. Welch for her father's postcards from Camp Cooke's Korean War–era days.

Joe Valencia's two books and photographs from the 1977 Honda Canyon fire captured a very sad time in Vandenberg's history. I am indebted to him for the photos of the fire. Thanks to artist Tim Gagnon for his donation of the STS-62A patch images.

Thanks to my parents, Joe and Kathy, for encouraging questioning and the search for wisdom. This drive has served me well.

As always, thanks to "my" baristas who kept the caffeine flowing—Kiesha, Taylor, Paul, Karrie, and Kayla.

Finally, I'd like to thank my tribe for allowing me to write this book, and eternal love to my wife, Kim.

Unless otherwise credited, all photographs are courtesy of the United States Air Force.

Introduction

In many ways, the eyes of the world have been on this scant 45 miles of California coastline for centuries. The Chumash peoples roamed the hills and valleys of the Santa Barbara Channel area for millennia, long before the Spanish conquistador Juan Cabrillo arrived in 1542. Spanish expeditions through the area began in 1769, with Gaspar de Portola's expedition through what is now Vandenberg, heading toward Monterey. The colonization of Alta California was a joint venture between the Catholic Church and the Spanish Crown, which included the construction of a series of missions in the region for the inculcation of church values onto the indigenous population. The original mission in the area, Mission La Purisima Conception, was created in 1787. By 1803, the Chumash had been removed from the village of Nocto and moved to La Purisima—boosting its population to over 1,500. After the Mexican government began secularizing the mission system in 1833, the lands were divided into 11 secular ranches, totaling over 200,000 acres from land grants, which were given to loyal subjects.

Throughout the rest of the 1800s, the lands remained as rural ranches that celebrated the area's Spanish heritage. The Southern Pacific Railroad was completed in 1896, linking San Francisco and Los Angeles for passengers and cargo.

In 1901, the area saw the US Lighthouse Service build a lighthouse in the vicinity of Point Arguello. In 1911, the original tower was replaced with a standalone tower. Even with the lighthouse positioned on the point, however, the US Navy had its largest peacetime disaster on September 8, 1923, at Point Pednerales—also known as Honda Point.

On that evening, seven destroyers—the USS *Delphy* (DD-261), USS *S.P. Lee* (DD-310), USS *Young* (DD-312), USS *Woodbury* (DD-309), USS *Nicholas* (DD-311), USS *Fuller* (DD-297), and USS *Chauncey* (DD-296)—while traveling at 20 knots, ran aground at Honda Point a few miles from the northern side of the Santa Barbara Channel off Point Arguello on the coast in Santa Barbara County, California. Two other ships grounded, but were able to maneuver free of the rocks. Twenty-three sailors died in the disaster.

Accounts of the Honda Point disaster demonstrate that many actions were taken that seem inconceivable almost a century later. US Naval Historical Center records state that:

> Just over twelve hours earlier, Destroyer Squadron ELEVEN (DesRon 11) left San Francisco Bay and formed up for a morning of combat maneuvers. In an important test of engineering efficiency, this was followed by a twenty-knot run south, including a night passage through the Santa Barbara Channel. In late afternoon, the fourteen destroyers fell into column formation, led by their flagship, USS Delphy. Poor visibility ensured that squadron commander Captain Edward H. Watson and two other experienced navigators on board Delphy had to work largely by the time-honored, if imprecise, technique of dead reckoning. Soundings could not be taken at twenty knots, but they checked their chartwork against bearings obtained from the radio direction finding (RDF) station at Point Arguello, a few miles south of Honda. At the time they expected to turn into the Channel, the Point Arguello station reported they were still to the northward. However, RDF was still new and not completely trusted, so this information was discounted, and DesRon 11 was ordered to turn eastward, with each ship following Delphy.

However, the Squadron was actually several miles north, and further east, than Delphy's navigators believed. It was very dark, and almost immediately the ships entered a dense fog. About five minutes after making her turn, Delphy slammed into the Honda shore and stuck fast. A few hundred yards astern, USS S.P. Lee saw the flagship's sudden stop and turned sharply to port, but quickly struck the hidden coast to the north of Delphy. Following her, USS Young had no time to turn before she ripped her hull open on submerged rocks, came to a stop just south of Delphy and rapidly turned over on her starboard side. The next two destroyers in line, Woodbury and Nicholas, turned right and left respectively, but also hit the rocks.

A special Court of Inquiry investigated the loss of twenty-three irreplaceable lives and seven expensive destroyers. A subsequent Court Martial adjudicated the issue of blame and punishment. Squadron Commander Edward H. Watson and the Commanding officers of Delphy and Nicholas were found guilty, though the latter's conviction was set aside by the reviewing Admiral.

The mid-1930s saw such an increase in coastal shipping that the Lighthouse Service built a lifeboat station. On July 1, 1939, the Lighthouse Service was combined with the Coast Guard, augmenting the service by 8,000 men and forming the corps that mans present-day light stations and navigation aid stations. During the interim of World War II, the Coast Guard manned Point Arguello Light and Point Arguello Lifeboat station, as well as a newly established LORAN station. In 1958, after 12 years of operation following the war, the Point Arguello Lifeboat Station was retired. Additional Navy activities in the area continued after World War II.

The mesa's military occupation continued during World War II, when the Army acquired 92,000 acres of California coastlands—from Point Sal to Point Arguello. In early 1941, military leaders planned to use areas within Santa Barbara County for training, due to favorable climate, terrain, and the proximity of the ocean. On June 5, 1941, the War Department gave the go-ahead for construction of a training camp on Burton Mesa and started purchasing 122 tracts of land, totaling 92,000 acres.

The planned training base was named Camp Cooke, after Gen. Philip St. George Cooke—an Army cavalry officer who was well known for his exploits during the Mexican-American War. General Cooke, whose military career spanned almost half a century, graduated from West Point in 1827 and retired in 1873. He participated in the Mexican War, the Indian Wars, and the Civil War. A native of Virginia, Cooke remained loyal to the Union during the Civil War. Perhaps his most enduring achievement, however, came when he was a colonel during the Mexican War and led a battalion of Mormons from Missouri to California. The route followed by Colonel Cooke in 1847 was opened as the first wagon route to California; today, the railroad follows much of the route of the early wagon trails.

After World War II, Camp Cooke was moved to inactive status in 1946. When the Korean War broke out in 1950, the camp was reopened to train tank crews. The 13th and 20th Armored Divisions, along with the 40th, 44th, 86th, and 91st Infantry Divisions, trained at Camp Cooke. The beach environment at Point Sal and Purisima Point proved useful for the practice of amphibious landings. After the camp's second deactivation in 1953, its 86,000 acres were maintained on a standby basis by Army Disciplinary Barracks personnel. The cantonment area of the base became overgrown with weeds, and the buildings fell into disrepair. To reduce the risk of fire, the Army allowed shepherds to keep their flocks on the base to thin out the brush.

In 1957, the secretary of defense directed the transfer of 64,000 acres of Camp Cooke from the Department of the Army to the Air Force, for the establishment of the free world's first missile base. On April 23, 1957, Camp Cooke was officially re-designated as Cooke Air Force Base, under the command of Col. David K. Lyster. Sixteen days later, the first ground-breaking ceremonies were held for the construction of a missile training center. A formal dedication was given by Brig. Gen. Osmond J. Ritland, vice commander of the Air Force Ballistic Missile Division. General Ritland spoke plainly about the base's importance to national security: "The primary mission of

Cooke AFB is the . . . training [of] Air Force units to include both Intermediate Range Ballistic Missiles (IRBM) and Intercontinental Ballistic Missiles (ICBM). A secondary mission [of the base] is to provide an operational capability for the ICBM."

Upon arrival to the base, Air Force personnel were given an introduction packet to Cooke AFB, which included established duty hours (0730–1630) from Monday to Friday, and a prescribed uniform schedule for summer and winter (May 15–November 14, and November 15–May 14, respectively). As the base was building up to operational standards, personnel from other missile launching bases, such as Cape Canaveral and the White Sands Missile Range, were brought in for their expertise in rocket science.

The name of Cooke AFB did not last long. The base was renamed Vandenberg Air Force Base in honor of the late Gen. Hoyt S. Vandenberg—second chief of staff of the United States Air Force, and chief architect of today's modern Air Force. The base's fact sheet details the personal history of General Vandenberg:

"Hoyt Vandenberg was born in Milwaukee, Wisconsin, on 24 January 1899. In 1923, he graduated from West Point Academy, ranking 240 in a class of 261. Vandenberg excelled in pilot training at both Brooks and Kelly Field in Texas. He flew attack and fighter aircraft and served two tours as an instructor pilot. His reputation as an outstanding pilot enabled him to obtain a series of education assignments at the Air Corps Tactical School, Maxwell AFB, Alabama; the Command and General Staff College, Fort Leavenworth, Kansas; and the Army War College, Washington, D.C.

In June 1939, he was assigned to the plans division of the office of the chief of the Air Corps. After the United States had entered World War II, he was appointed operations and training officer of the Air Staff under General Henry H. (Hap) Arnold. During the early stages of the war, Vandenberg (then a colonel), was transferred to England and assisted in planning air operations for the invasion of North Africa. He received his first star in December 1942, and became chief of staff of the Twelfth Air Force in North Africa under General James H. Doolittle. During this campaign he flew over two dozen combat missions over Tunisia, Italy, Sardinia, Sicily, and Panteileria to obtain firsthand information.

In March 1945, he was promoted to the rank of lieutenant general, and full general in 1947. Meanwhile, in January 1946, General Vandenberg was appointed chief of the intelligence division of the General Staff. In June, he was named director of the Central Intelligence Group, predecessor to the Central Intelligence Agency formed in 1947.

He returned to duty with the Air Force in May 1947, and became deputy commander and chief of staff of the Army Air Force. With the establishment of a separate Air Force in September 1947, Vandenberg became its first vice chief of staff under General Carl Spaatz, and succeeded him on 30 April 1948. He held that post through the critical periods of the Berlin airlift (1948-1949) and the Korean War (1950-1953).

Weak, exhausted, and in constant pain from cancer, General Vandenberg retired from the Air Force in June 1953. He died in Washington, D.C. on 2 April 1954. In honor of his service to the nation, the aerospace base at Lompoc, California, formerly Cooke Air Force Base, was renamed Vandenberg Air Force Base on 4 October 1958."

At the base, the pressure to complete missile research and developmental test launches was immense. All the hard work was validated on December 16, 1958, however. The first missile launched at Vandenberg AFB was a Thor IRBM, which completed a successful mission into a Pacific Ocean target area. Immediately after the first West Coast launch of an Atlas-D ICBM, Commander in Chief for Strategic Air Command (SAC) Gen. Thomas S. Power declared the Atlas system operational.

America's first ICBM unit, the 576th Strategic Missile Squadron, was activated on April 1, 1958. The unit was assigned the SM-65 Atlas D missile, and the first missile with a live nuclear warhead went on strategic alert on October 31, 1959. Over the course of seven years, the 576th would launch all variants of the Atlas. By the end of 1959, thirteen missile complexes had been built—seven Thor IRBM pads, six Atlas ICBM locations, and seven Titan I silos.

In addition to providing missile testing and operational training, Vandenberg featured several geographic characteristics that ideally fit the space and missile launch missions. South-facing Purisima Point offered a launch site that sent rockets into space without crossing over any land mass until Antarctica, and was the only possible location for this unique type of launch in the continental United States. Specifically defined as a polar orbit, this orbit provided worldwide coverage every 24 hours and originated an interesting offshoot of the space age: the reconnaissance (or "spy") satellite.

The National Reconnaissance Program was created on September 6, 1961, and gave birth to the ultra-secretive National Reconnaissance Office (NRO). One of the first programs run under the NRP was the Corona family of satellites. Names such as Corona, Argon, Lanyard, Quill, Gambit, and Hexagon were spoken in hushed tones by Vandenberg personnel during the early days of the Cold War. The Corona series consisted of three versions; the codename "Keyhole" (KH) was retroactively assigned to distinguish between the different versions. The KH-1 carried a single-camera, single-recovery capsule, as did the KH-2 and KH-3. The KH-4 carried one recovery capsule, also known as a "film bucket," but featured a dual-camera system; and the KH-4A and KH-4B carried dual cameras and two recovery buckets. While official histories show the net result of the NRP's early efforts, the early days of Corona were wrought with uncertainty linked to the reliability of both booster and satellite.

In this program, ingenuity and derring-do were required in spades. In one famous story from the NRO's official Corona history, a fix was required for an overheating problem. According to Oder, Fitzpatrick, and Worthman's history of Corona: "In order to contain the water and prevent sloshing, something absorbent, soft, and easy to work with was required. After conducting a test program on various materials, the design engineer chose sanitary napkins '. . . because.' "

By the time of KH-8 Gambit-3 and KH-9 Hexagon launches, space launches had become routine, so less daring (and presumably more classified) methods were used to solve sticky technological problems.

Vandenberg's dichotomy during the Cold War is aptly summed up in the 1985 anti-war ballad "Russians," by the rock star Sting. While Khrushchev's nuclear forces did not "bury" the United States, the promise of protection from President Reagan's Strategic Defense Initiative (the "Star Wars" system) did not come to fruition either. Launching missiles gave military planners interesting applications to problems, such as observing missile launches. During the Gemini 5 mission, astronauts Ed White and Pete Conrad viewed the launch of a Minuteman missile from Vandenberg, validating the use of humans for intelligence gathering from space.

The Advanced Ballistic Re-Entry System (ABRES) program gave new life to retired first-generation ICBMs such as the Atlas. The same gantries and control centers that housed and monitored on-alert missiles in the late 1950s were used to launch ICBMs with prototype reentry vehicles, testing various designs and materials for optimum performance. After Atlas, the 1970s brought the retired Minuteman I missiles into the ABRES program as test boosters.

For past and present missile combat crewmembers, commonly known as "missileers," Vandenberg occupies a special place of honor as a service posting, as it was the sole location for missile combat crew training. In 1964, Secretary of Defense Robert McNamara limited the Minuteman force to 1,000 missiles, comprising 20 squadrons divided between six strategic missile wings (Malmstrom, Ellsworth, Minot, Whiteman, FE Warren, and Grand Forks AFBs). Crews from the six wings would arrive at Vandenberg for Follow-on Test and Evaluation (FOT&E) launches, known as Glory Trips, to validate weapon system parameters.

The base's legacy throughout the decades can hardly be contained in any one volume of literature, let alone the scant paragraphs above. Regardless of the reader's area of interest, Vandenberg AFB's geographic expanse, varied wildlife and exploration sites, and depth of history can only reinforce the base's legacy in the history of the national security of the United States.

One
THE RANCHERO ERA AND CAMP COOKE (1542–1958)

Spanish expeditions through the area did not start with Juan Bautista de Anza's group, but records of his journey through California's central coast managed to identify two campsites on current-day Vandenberg property. Later centuries saw teeming ranches, stemming from land grants given to loyal subjects by the Spanish government.

Off the coast, the rich maritime heritage of the area is rife with centuries of shipwrecks. The Navy's greatest peacetime tragedy took place in September 1923, at an isolated feature locally known as Honda Point. Officially called Point Pedernales, it is the northern entrance to the heavily trafficked Santa Barbara Channel. Buffeted by wind and often obscured by fog, this rocky shore has claimed many vessels over time—but never more in one stroke than at 9:00 p.m. on the evening of September 8, 1923. Seven US Navy destroyers ran aground there, and 23 lives were lost.

The 1940s saw the Central Coast prepare to engage in World War II. The Department of War established Camp Cooke on October 5, 1941, and the subsequent months saw a substantial increase in personnel and materiel being moved to the location. Additionally, a prisoner of war camp was built within the cantonment, operating from June 16, 1944, until May 18, 1946. Camp Cooke was closed in June 1946, and put into caretaker status until it reopened to support training for the Korean War—training two armored divisions (the 13th and 20th) and four infantry divisions (the 40th, 44th, 86th, and 91st). After the conflict ended, the camp was again closed in February 1953. Later studies conducted by the Air Force singled out the site as an ideal location for a guided missile training base and space launch site. After its transfer from the Army in 1957, the base was renamed Cooke Air Force Base.

The Chumash tribe has inhabited the lands surrounding Vandenberg for over 10,000 years. In many locations, they painted intricate, finely crafted images on reflective rock surfaces created by ancient volcanic flows. The colors used for the Honda Ridge pictographs were derived from hematite, giving the images a reddish tint. To allow visitors to view the images, the base created a protective enclave upon Tranquillion Ridge, on South Vandenberg.

The wreck of the *Sybil Marsten* lays right off the coast of present-day Surf Beach. The steam-powered ship, with its cargo of 1.25 million board feet of lumber, ran aground on January 12, 1909, after confusing the train depot lights with the Point Arguello Lighthouse. The cargo spread across the beach, and was salvaged by Lompoc residents. Two entrepreneurs even recovered enough wood to start their own lumber yard. (Lompoc Valley Historical Society.)

Stranded on Honda Point on May 28, 1933, the SS *Nippon Maru* ran aground at the exact same location as the USS *Fuller* did during the Navy disaster of 1923. The ship was a World War I "Z-class" tanker and ran afoul of the weather and navigational errors common to Point Pednerales. The wreck was floated, salvaged, and abandoned to the sea several months later. (Lompoc Valley Historical Society.)

The SS *Orowaite* wrecked at Point Sal in August 1924. The *Orowaite* was a British steamship on a voyage from Wellington, New Zealand, to Port San Luis to pick up cargo. After the accident, the British Consulate Naval Court exonerated the captain, finding that the stranding was due to an unusual southeasterly set and low visibility at the time of the accident. (Lompoc Valley Historical Society.)

Known as the "Boathouse," this building on Point Arguello is actually the administration building and barracks of the former Coast Guard station. The building was constructed in a two-year period, from 1936 to 1938, and conducted rescue operations until the US Coast Guard decommissioned the station on September 8, 1952. The real boathouse was demolished in 1982 to make way for the Space Shuttle program at Vandenberg. (National Park Service.)

Around Point Arguello, heading towards Sudden Ranch, a pier juts out near the jetty. During its heyday, this rescue station had a four-man crew ready 24 hours a day. The rescue crew had ten minutes from the sounding of the lookout alarm to launch into the sea. If ships wrecked on the rocky shoals, the crew also had a truck-mounted brass cannon that could shoot a rescue line nearly a mile. (National Park Service.)

In 1918, rancher Edwin Marshall and his son Marcus started the Casmalia Ranch and Cattle Company. The Marshalls also managed Rancho Jesus Maria, traveling from Los Angeles to the central coast every weekend. Apiaries, cattle, chickens, and turkeys were just a few of the types of livestock tended in the area. The elder Marshall also grew eucalyptus for firewood, which had the added benefit of providing breaks against the punishing coastal wind. (Lompoc Valley Historical Society.)

Edwin Marshall named his guest house "Marshallia," after a genus of plants in the family *Asteraceae* that are not endemic to the Central Coast area. However, Marshallia stuck as the nickname for the entire ranch. After Marshall's death in 1937, the ranch was used as a recreation site by the Hollywood movie star crowd. The military continued this by using the site as housing for high-ranking officers, and as a golf course. (Lompoc Valley Historical Society.)

The wreckage of the USS *Chauncey* (DD-296) lies grounded among the rocks at Point Pedernales. The *Chauncey* was the last ship grounded, as it was the last in line of Destroyer Division 31. As it was stranded upright and suffered no loss of men, the *Chauncey*'s crew immediately went to the aid of the nearby USS *Young* (DD 312), which had capsized. Wreckage from the *Chauncey* still can be spotted during negative low tides. (Naval Historical Center.)

The wreckage of the *S.P. Lee* (DD 310) and *Nicholas* (DD 311) lay near the cliffs. The crew of the *S.P. Lee*, along with the *Delphy*'s, had to climb up the sharp rock face, injuring themselves in the process. The USS *Nicholas*' crew had to wait until the following day before abandoning ship. (Naval Historical Center.)

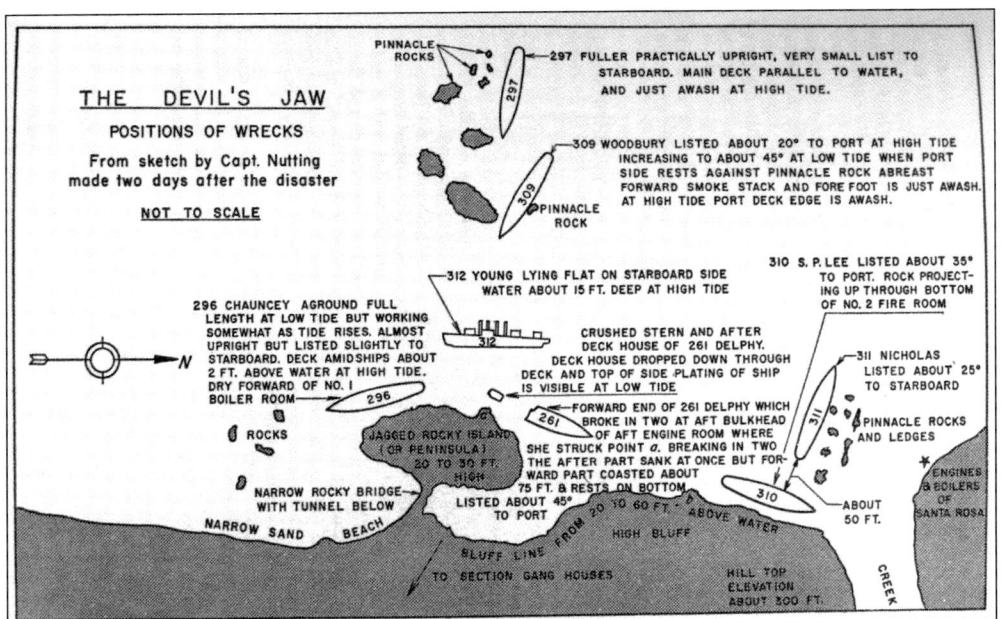

This map of the Honda Point disaster shows the specific orientation of, and detailed information on, the unlucky ships as they came around Point Pedernales on the evening of September 8, 1923. (Naval Historical Center.)

In this photograph, more ship wreckage lies off Honda Point. The Naval Historical Center's study on the Honda Point disaster stated that "[when] the closest-in ship's crews had reached land, the sound of a train whistle revealed that they were really on the mainland, and not miles away on San Miguel island. In fact, the Southern Pacific's coastal railway line, with a well-staffed maintenance section house, was less than a half-mile inland." The proximity of the rail line helped in evacuating casualties. (Naval Historical Center.)

This image—looking northwest from the shore—shows the USS *Chauncey*, grounded, with wreckage a few yards to the west. (Naval Historical Center.)

This drawing of the Devil's Jaw shows the wreckage looking towards the shore. The Southern Pacific Railroad trestle over Honda Creek can be seen at the upper left, looking much as it does today. (Naval Historical Center.)

These two postcards from Camp Cooke's early years show illustrations of California Boulevard, a recreation hall and barracks, and division headquarters, as well as some other points of interest to garrison residents. These two cards were collected by Pfc. Cletus M. Welch, 375th Military Police Company, during his assignment to Camp Cooke as a guard at the US Disciplinary Barracks (1951–1952). Sixty years later, his daughter Dianne, herself a retired veteran of the Air Force, worked at the base library and assisted with the research for this book. (Dianne Welch.)

Camp Cooke was named after Gen. Philip St. George Cooke, who is sometimes called the "Father of the US Cavalry." During the Mexican-American War, Cooke—then a lieutenant colonel—led the famed Mormon Battalion through the Southwestern United States to San Diego. During the Civil War, Cooke remained in the Army while his son John Rogers Cooke and son-in-law J.E.B. Stuart fought for the Confederacy. (Library of Congress.)

Here, the American flag is being raised at Camp Cooke's main parade ground, while the nearby Purisima Hills can be clearly seen in the background. The camp was activated as an infantry and armor training center in October 1941, after the War Department had purchased 122 tracts of land. The land tracts varied in size from the 0.009 acres of the L.C. Sanor tract to the 40,930 acres of Jesus Maria Rancho. (Lompoc Valley Historical Society.)

In this photograph, pup tents have been lined up at Camp Cooke during World War II training activities. Life on Burton Mesa was difficult for the first few months after the camp's establishment. Dust, mud, fog, and wind were a constant presence for the training soldiers. The weather provided an obstacle to construction crews in the early months, and a nuisance to the training soldiers. (Lompoc Valley Historical Society.)

Soldiers at the camp often enjoyed time at the USO. The camp's distance from large cities posed a unique problem: soldiers would be "homebodies" and stay on the military reservation. This increased the demand for entertainment, shows, athletic events, and other pleasant distractions. In the wartime history of Camp Cooke, Sgt. Wesley W. Purkiss noted that "[Camp Cooke had] more athletic facilities than any other camp in the country." (Lompoc Valley Historical Society.)

Here, a soldier sifts through the camp's tin recycling pile. The salvage and surplus section of the camp used labor from captured German prisoners of war in addition to the staffed GIs who processed material for sale back to the American public. The sales from salvaged materials in 1944 and 1945 averaged over $80,000. (Lompoc Valley Historical Society.)

After kitchen duty, a soldier gathers cooking fat. The camp's population hit a high in June 1943, with over 35,000 soldiers in garrison. The amount of food needed to feed an army of men that size is massive. For example: the popcorn sold at the camp's four theaters was ordered in 50 to 100-ton lots, along with 5,000 gallons of Mazola oil. (Lompoc Valley Historical Society.)

Here, a group of military police gather for a photograph. During the war years, the MPs at Camp Cooke had their hands full. A consolidated criminal investigation report from January 1944 to March 1946 tallied the following criminal acts: assault (33), arson (7), burglary (12), embezzlement, fraud or forgery (2), homicide (2), impersonations (2), liquor violations (3), robbery (19), sex offenses (21), stolen property (1), theft (72), and suicide (1). (Lompoc Valley Historical Society.)

This lieutenant in the Women's Army Corps (WAC) was a model before the war. A detachment of WACs was activated in April 1944 and was originally assigned as a hospital company. After the war ended, the arrival of the 13th and 20th Armored Divisions increased the demand for WACs to assist in other sections—from the motor pool to the hospital. (Lompoc Valley Historical Society.)

Here, a tank maneuvers through mud. Weapons used on the training ranges at Camp Cooke varied from small arms to machine guns, grenades, and rocket launchers. Many areas of present-day Vandenberg still have explosive ordnance disposal teams combing for unexploded ordnance left over from the Camp Cooke days. (Lompoc Valley Historical Society.)

In this photograph, a tank-mounted flamethrower shoots a fiery spray while soldiers look on. During the Korean War, mock villages were constructed to train soldiers in house-to-house fighting techniques. (Lompoc Valley Historical Society.)

After Camp Cooke's first closure in 1946, the cantonment fell into disuse and caretaker duties were transferred to the Army Disciplinary Barracks (the present day Federal Correctional Institution, Lompoc). The army leased the grounds to local farmers for agriculture and grazing lands for sheep. (Lompoc Valley Historical Society.)

Camp Cooke's second closure in 1953 saw a similar transfer of responsibility to the Disciplinary Barracks staff. Again, the garrison area fell into disrepair, and the same deal was struck with local shepherds to allow grazing to eliminate the weeds and keep the fire hazard low. A short four years later, the camp would find itself on the cutting edge of space technology as the vanguard site for both Space Race rockets and Cold War missiles. (Lompoc Valley Historical Society.)

Hoyt Sanford Vandenberg was born in Milwaukee, Wisconsin, on January 24, 1899. In 1923, he graduated from West Point, ranking 240th in a class of 261. He became chief of staff of the North West African Strategic Air Force during World War II, earning the Silver Star, Distinguished Flying Cross, and Legion of Merit for missions flown under hostile fire. He later helped plan the Normandy Invasion (Operation Overlord).

Here, Hoyt Vandenberg III, the grandson of Gen. Hoyt S. Vandenberg, is being presented a missile badge by Gen. Mark Wade, 1st Missile Division commander, during the base's renaming ceremony on October 4, 1958.

Pictured here on October 4, 1958, Capt. Hoyt S. Vandenberg Jr. and Gladys Rose Vandenberg are seen standing at the main gate's entry sign. Cooke AFB was renamed after the second chief of staff of the Air Force (1948–1953), Gen. Hoyt S. Vandenberg. He died in Washington, DC, on April 2, 1954, and was buried at Arlington National Cemetery. General Vandenberg was survived by his wife, Gladys Rose Vandenberg; his daughter, Gloria Miller; and son, retired Maj. Gen. Hoyt S. Vandenberg Jr.

Soon after the base renaming ceremony, an unidentified worker placed the finishing touches on the Pine Canyon Gate sign of the newly christened Vandenberg Air Force Base.

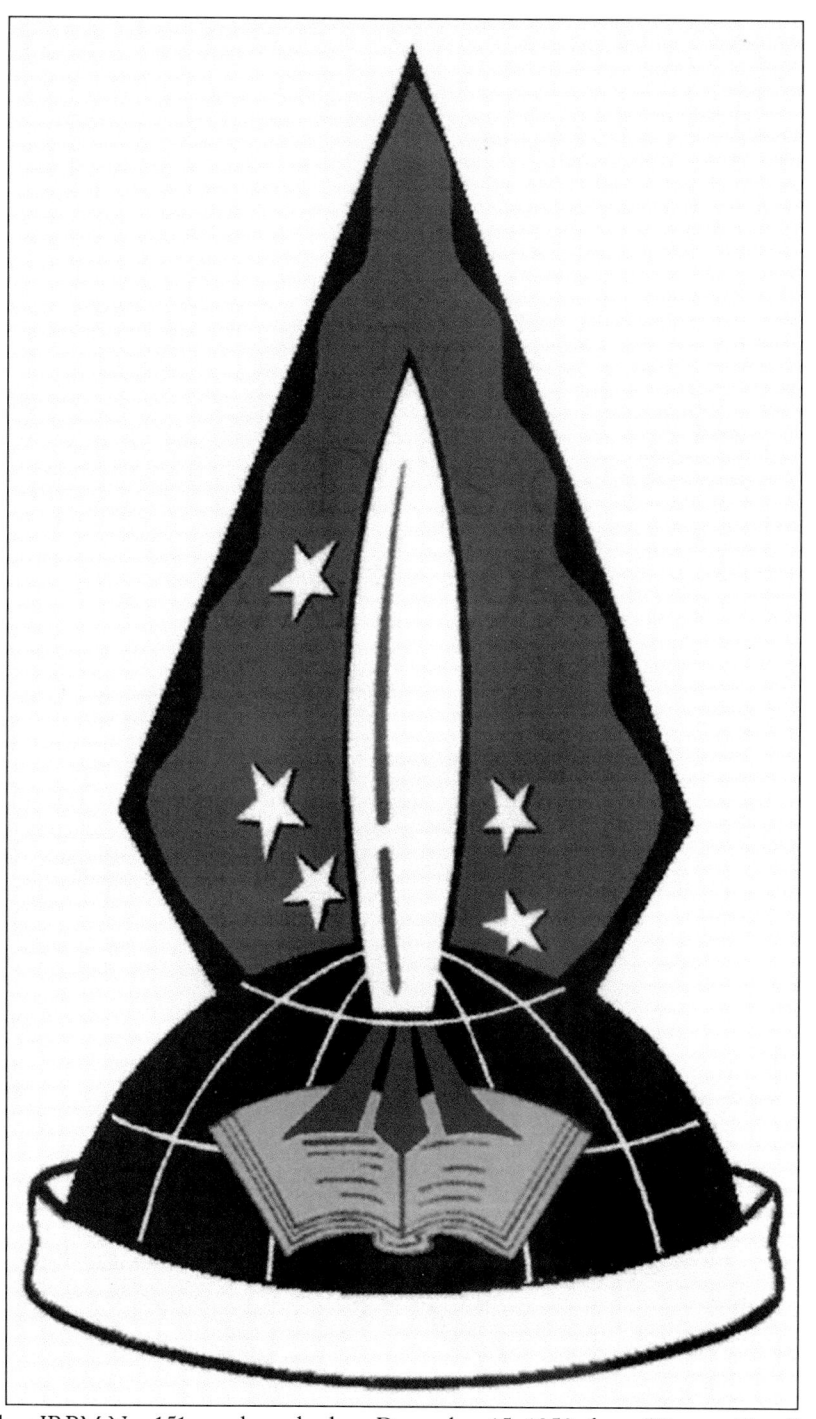

SM-75 Thor IRBM No. 151 was launched on December 15, 1958, from Western Test Range pad 75-1-1, the first missile launched at Vandenberg. The test, nicknamed "Tune Up," was authorized by Launch Order 301-75-58, was the first launch performed by a SAC missile crew, and was led by missileer Capt. Bennie Castillo. The test was an unheralded success for the base, its personnel, and the nation.

Two

EARLY DAYS OF THE COLD WAR (1959–1976)

The first two decades after Vandenberg's establishment saw monumental changes to the base as its operating environment expanded into outer space. Construction during the early part of the 1960s concentrated on first-generation missile systems, such as Thor, Atlas, and Titan, to meet the national security demands of intermediate-range ballistic missiles (IRBMs) and intercontinental ballistic missiles (ICBMs). The two commands responsible for the missiles, Air Research and Development Command (ARDC) and Strategic Air Command (SAC), worked hand-in-hand to provide the best systems, and expertly trained crews for missile duty around the United States.

During the tumultuous days of the early 1960s, SAC maintained five different missile systems at Vandenberg. Rockets and missiles launched on a near-weekly basis. In fact, during 1962–1963, there was a launch approximately every three days. These missiles were launched frequently for developmental testing, to work out problems, and allow for follow-on evaluations. As systems matured and became more reliable, they were modified into space launch vehicles for civil and military uses.

A quintessential Cold War figure, Pres. John F. Kennedy made an appearance at Vandenberg on March 23, 1962. During his visit, President Kennedy watched an Atlas-D launch, saw models of high-tech spacecraft, visited a Minuteman silo, and was made an honorary missile-man. His visit to Vandenberg helped cement the absolute trust given to US missile forces.

The latter half of the decade saw the normalization of space and missile activities. Missile operations had become routine. To keep on the cutting edge, SAC headquarters initiated a friendly competition to increase proficiency and camaraderie among the nine missile wings (six Minuteman and three Titan II). As the training location for all ICBM crews, Vandenberg seemed the natural place to hold the competition. In 1967, the first missile competition, codenamed "Curtain Raiser," was held at locations around Vandenberg. Next year's competition was cancelled due to the Vietnam War, but the competition—later renamed "Olympic Arena"—continued until the end of the Cold War in 1992.

The logo of the 576th Strategic Missile Squadron incorporates elements from its parent organization, Strategic Air Command. The missile reflects the squadron's mission, while the steel mail fist represents strength atop a globe and the lightning bolts represent rapid global reach. The olive branches subtly reinforce SAC's motto "Peace is our Profession." The 576th's motto "Ducimus"—Latin for "We Lead"—was appropriate for America's first ICBM organization, activated on April 1, 1958. (Air Force Historical Research Agency.)

The first Atlas launch from Vandenberg was Atlas 12D, on September 9, 1959, from Western Test Range complex 576 A-2. The missile program began in 1946 as MX-774 but was cancelled by a cash-strapped military in 1947. The project was restarted as MX-1593 in January 1951 and named Atlas. From this operational configuration would stem ICBMs, satellite launch vehicles, manned spaceflight launch vehicles, and ballistic missile defense targets.

The first Thor missile was launched by a British Royal Air Force crew on April 16, 1959, codenamed "Lions Roar." The launch was observed by Air Vice-Marshals W.C. Sheen and Sir Augustus Walker of the Ministry of Defense. RAF crews trained at Vandenberg under the 392nd Missile Training Squadron alongside SAC crews. The first eight-week integrated weapons system training course began on March 2, 1959, with 133 students.

A Handley Page Victor strategic bomber flies over this Thor missile at SLC-10. Project Emily was the name of the program that deployed Thor missiles to the United Kingdom. To meet the rapid deployment timeline, many aspects of the program were taken from the Atlas program. The Mark 2 reentry vehicle with W-49 warhead, the Rocketdyne engine, and the all-inertial guidance system were used to meet the planned initial operating capability date in December 1959.

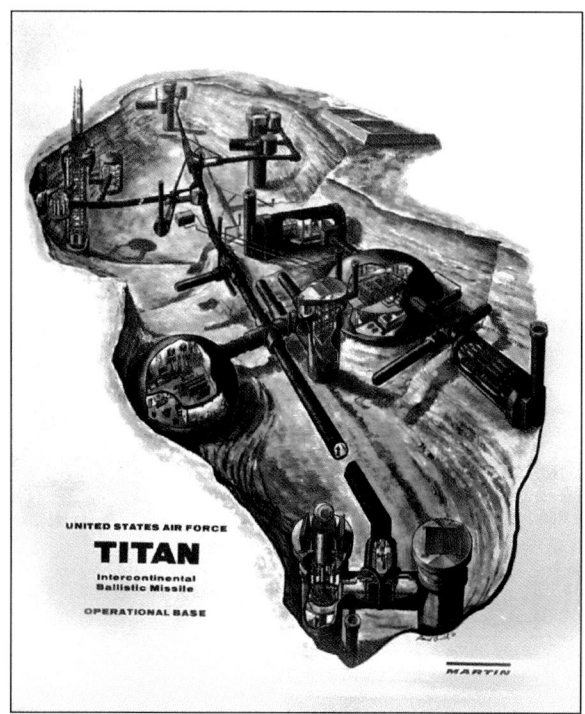

Each HGM-25A Titan I complex contained three missile launchers, as shown here, which were laced together by an intricate network of steel tunnels. Vandenberg's Titan I site, 395A, was the first underground missile launch complex in the United States. The Titan I force of 54 missiles was contained within 18 complexes (similar in layout and size to 395A) spread over five states: Colorado, California, South Dakota, Idaho, and Washington. (Lockheed Martin Corporation.)

A view from inside the Complex 395A tunnels shows the detail of the underground steel tubes and cable runs. Construction of the site uncovered problems unique to building underground structures. Methane pockets had to be emptied and electrical grounding issues—caused by corrosion from the increased salinity inside the rock—had to be solved. The path to finding solutions during 395A's construction would bolster the follow-on silo construction efforts of the Titan I and II, Atlas-F, and Minuteman programs.

As the first silo-based system, the SM-68 Titan I required a robust infrastructure and underground space requirements that seemed equal to a small city. The first-generation ICBMs, Atlas and Titan, were not fully hardened against a nuclear blast. The lifespan of the SM-68 Titan I missile was a little under ten years—from contract signing with the Martin Company on October 27, 1955, to the final missile being taken off alert on April 1, 1965.

An accident occurred at the Titan Operational Suitability Test Facility (OSTF) on December 3, 1960. A full rehearsal—short of an actual launch—was successfully conducted. After the test, however, the missile and elevator fell to the bottom of the silo and ignited propellant and oxidizers. Over 160 tons of structural steel flew out of the silo. The blast obliterated the OSTF, throwing debris as far as a mile.

Project Sky Rocket was the codename for Pres. John F. Kennedy's visit to Vandenberg AFB on March 23, 1962. Kennedy's visit, complete with entourage and limousine as shown here, lasted a little less than three hours, before he departed for Palm Springs. To date, President Kennedy is the only American president to visit Vandenberg. (John F. Kennedy Presidential Library and Museum.)

Here, Pres. Kennedy (left) exits the complex 576B Launch Control Center with Gen. Thomas S. Power. Secretary of Defense Robert McNamara is seen to Kennedy's left, over his shoulder. (John F. Kennedy Presidential Library and Museum.)

During his visit, President Kennedy greeted the missile combat crew of the Atlas 134 launch. Crew R-07 (seen here in white) consisted of, from left to right, Maj. Clifford W. Simonson (MCCC), Capt. Kenneth E. Haithcoat (GEO), M.Sgt. William J. Chupka (BMAT), S.Sgt. Roger R. Egert (BMAS), S.Sgt. Reginald E. Bufkin (MER), S.Sgt. Dale M. Howe (MPR), S.Sgt. Sherman L. Jackson (MEM), S.Sgt. Gerald G. Beth (RTST), S.Sgt. Arnold E. Kovakka (EDDFR), A1C John W. Hill (MMT), and A1C Franklin D. Waters (RTSS). (John F. Kennedy Presidential Library and Museum.)

After the launch of Atlas-134D, Maj. Simonson stated, "Mr. President, as a token of your attendance at this Atlas launch today, I am honored to present this personal missile badge on behalf of our Strategic Air Command missile combat crews." For Major Simonson, the presidential missile launch was one of the highlights of his career, positively supporting President Kennedy's decision to expand the land-based ICBM program after the successful launch. (John F. Kennedy Presidential Library and Museum.)

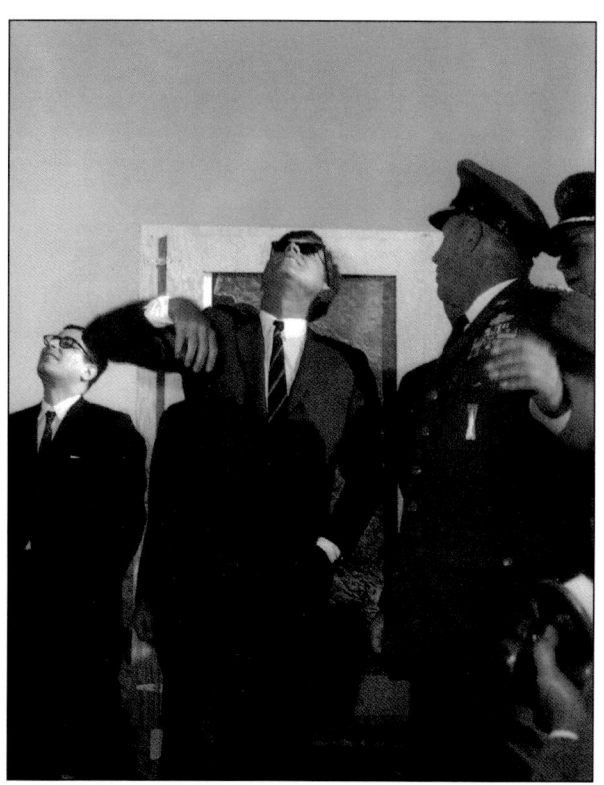

Here, President Kennedy (center) looks skyward at the Atlas-134 launch—codenamed Curry Comb I—as head of Strategic Air Command, Gen. Thomas S. Power (right), describes the launch procedure and the missile's destination in the Pacific Ocean. (John F. Kennedy Presidential Library and Museum.)

As President Kennedy (left) and General Power (right) watch Atlas-134 reach skyward, Secretary of Defense Robert S. McNamara can be seen in the background between them. The launch successfully delivered the Mark 3 Mod IIIB reentry vehicle 4,300 miles downrange, into the Marshall Islands. (John F. Kennedy Presidential Library and Museum.)

In this photograph, President Kennedy (center, in sunglasses) views a Minuteman I launch facility and transporter erector vehicle during his visit. (John F. Kennedy Presidential Library and Museum.)

The Automatic Program Checkout Crew (APCHE) from the 389th Missile Maintenance Squadron prepared the Atlas-134 missile for launch. Pictured from left to right are (first row), 1st Lt. Donald B. Kirby, A2C Douglas H. Turner (MMT), S.Sgt. David H. Dixon (MEM)), A1C Kenneth R. Pierson, and T.Sgt. John Gilbert (BMAT); (second row) S.Sgt. Donald P. Klein (MMT), A1C Jerry D. Brown (MPT), A1C William Farley, and A1C John McCutcheon (MET).

An Army Corps of Engineers sign near Point Sal bears the name "WS-133A – Point Sal Area Utilities Phase 1." This refers to the Minuteman ICBM project. According to Col. Charles Terhune in *Ace in the Hole: the Story of the Minuteman Missile,* Lt. Col. Ed Hall conceived of the name "Sentinel" for the system, but Gen. Bernard Schriever renamed it Minuteman to create a connection to the American Revolutionary War's iconic citizen-soldiers.

These underground Minuteman command and control facilities—the Launch Control Center and the Launch Control Equipment Building—were constructed with concrete and reinforcement bars that could withstand the 1,000 pounds per square inch produced by a near-miss blast. Later Soviet weapons would sport higher blast yields and greater accuracy, forcing planners to develop an alternative means to launch the Minuteman ICBM force through the Airborne Launch Control System.

These workmen are inspecting the launch facility's reinforcement bars prior to concrete encapsulation and protection from 300-psi blasts. The Minuteman missiles were built because SAC desired a dispersed force of missiles that were ready to launch at a moment's notice. The solid fuel downstages allowed for round the clock readiness, and the dispersal and hardness of the launch facilities were designed to prevent the Soviets from destroying many strategic sites with a relatively small number of incoming missiles.

A prefabricated, solid steel Launcher Equipment Room is carried along Point Sal road towards North Base. The semi-circular object sits alongside the launch tube containing the missile, allowing maintenance personnel access to electronic equipment feeding data to the missile guidance set—the brains of the missile.

Framed against the main gate's rock sign, a salvo shot of two Minuteman missiles takes to the skies. Originally designated "Weapon System Q," the Minuteman would change designations many times: SM-80, HSM-80A/B, LGM-30A/B (Minuteman I), LGM-30F (Minuteman II), and LGM-30G (Minuteman III). Vandenberg would launch them all. As the decades passed and weapon systems were retired, salvo shots like this became less common.

This is a competition crew patch from the 1967 SAC Missile Combat Competition—codenamed Curtain Raiser. About the competition, Association of Air Force Missileers' executive director Col. Charles Simpson (ret.) stated, "In late 1966, CINCSAC announced plans for the first competition . . . to be conducted primarily at Vandenberg with some parts performed at Malmstrom AFB, Montana."

The Mesa Service Club proudly displayed a sign welcoming competitors to the 1967 SAC Missile Combat Competition. Curtain Raiser brought together two combat crews and one target and alignment team from each of the Minuteman and Titan II wings.

Taken the night before score posting, this picture of the leader board for 1967's Curtain Raiser missile competition shows no point standings for the nine competing missile wings. Since crew positions did not match up between the Titan II and Minuteman ICBM wings, separate categories existed for each system. The overall winner, decided using points and established weighting criteria, would take the Blanchard Trophy. In 1967, the 351st Strategic Missile Wing of Whiteman AFB, Missouri, won.

The Blanchard Trophy was a prize that most missile competitors longed for. Early versions of the trophy included a Minuteman I and Titan II model on the sides. The trophy was named after Gen. William H. Blanchard, who, at the time of his death on May 31, 1966, was serving as the Air Force vice chief of staff. The trophy was first awarded in 1967 and given to the best missile unit.

Space launch vehicles, developed from IRBMs and ICBMs, often took flight alongside their more lethal cousins. From this photograph of a Delta launch, the launcher's relation to the Thor IRBM is quite evident; from the ground support equipment and launch shelter, to the shape of the rocket core. The Delta family would be one of the most reliable launch systems in the United States, and remains in use today.

This Atlas-Agena booster, launched from SLC-3, carried a Gambit-1 satellite. Modifications to SLC-3 in 1963 allowed it to launch KH-4 Corona spy satellites atop Thor-Agena rockets. The complex was refurbished in 1973 to accommodate surplus Atlas ICBMs being used in a space launch role.

Workers pose in front of the launch gantry at SLC-3W in the mid-1960s. SLC-3 was one of the first operational installations in the US military space program. Until its destruction in 2000, SLC-3W contained the only remaining A-frame service gantry (mobile service towers), which were characteristic of early Atlas launch pad construction. (National Park Service.)

The idyllic setting of Sudden Ranch—seen here during SLC-6 construction in 1968—belies the struggle to obtain the lands of South Vandenberg. With Vandenberg's acquisition of Naval Missile Facility Point Arguello on July 1, 1964, the base encompassed almost all of the land from Point Sal to Point Arguello. The addition of the Sudden Ranch property in 1966 gave the Air Force the safety margin it needed to complete the Manned Orbiting Laboratory (MOL) heavy lift launch facility at SLC-6.

The flame ducts under SLC-6, seen here while under construction, would come back as an issue during the refurbishment of the space shuttle fleet in the 1980s. The MOL booster was a Titan IIIM (3M), which used a nitrogen tetroxide and Aerozine (a 50-50 mix of hydrazine and unsymmetrical dimethylhydrazine) storable propellant that was developed for use in the Titan II ICBM. The fuel was hypergolic and ignited on contact, with little worry of residual fuel ignition in the ducts.

The logo of the 395th Strategic Missile Squadron shows an ICBM reaching skyward, bordered by olive branches of peace that stem from a book of knowledge. The 395th SMS would perform 78 launches of both Titan I first generation and Titan II second generation ICBMs. Squadron members would remain on hand as contractors for the Titan II, Titan III, and Titan IV space launch vehicle program, sharing their knowledge.

Postcards of Vandenberg from the 1960s show the Marshallia Ranch golf course (top), the 1st Missile Division Headquarters (center), and a dinner at the base officer's club.

In a juxtaposition of new and old, this Atlas transporter rolls by the sign for the La Purisima mission park outside of Lompoc. During the early days, transportation routes to the base were limited for hauling large cargo, like a missile.

Three

EYES IN THE SKY

From the earliest days of the Cold War, national leaders were concerned about the possibility of a surprise attack on the United States—a sort of "nuclear Pearl Harbor." Millions of dollars were put toward early warning radar systems in the Arctic and along the coasts to warn of any surprise attack from the Soviet Union's air armada. The development of the ICBM replaced the lumbering aircraft threat with a rapid response weapon.

Created in 1961, the National Reconnaissance Office (NRO) took on the responsibilities of the National Reconnaissance Program (NRP), which consisted of airborne and spaceborne systems to monitor changes in the strategic balance between the United States and USSR. The unique circumstances of monitoring a landmass at very high northern latitudes by satellite was overcome with the polar orbit—allowing a satellite to circle over the North and South Poles. While in this orbit, the Earth below rotates at a constant rate, allowing the viewing of every inch of the globe over time.

Vandenberg's early claim to fame was as the only site in the United States that could allow a launch into polar orbit without the boost rocket flying over a populated area. A launch from the California coast doesn't fly over another landmass until Antarctica.

The world's first photoreconnaissance satellite, CORONA, took flight from Vandenberg AFB on February 28, 1959. It would take 13 launches before the first successful recovery of the reentry capsule. From 1959 to 1972, CORONA would amass 144 missions and collect over 800,000 images. The NRO would continue to use Vandenberg to launch follow-on reconnaissance systems, such as the now-declassified Quill, Lanyard, Gambit, Dorian, and Hexagon programs—as well as other systems that remain classified.

The list of firsts from the Corona program is impressive: first photoreconnaissance satellite in the world; first man-made object returned to Earth, first mid-air recovery of a vehicle returning from space, first mapping of the Earth from space, first stereo-optical data from space, first multiple reentry vehicles from space, first reconnaissance program to fly 100 missions, and first reconnaissance satellite program to be declassified. Contributions from other NRO programs, while equally impressive, will stay hidden for the foreseeable future.

The first Discoverer/Corona was launched on February 28, 1959, and became the first polar orbiting satellite. The booster carried an engineering payload of the Keyhole (KH) series, with no camera or film, and no recovery planned. No radio signals were received after launch, so its fate remains unknown. It is believed, however, that the satellite ended up near the South Pole. (National Reconnaissance Office.)

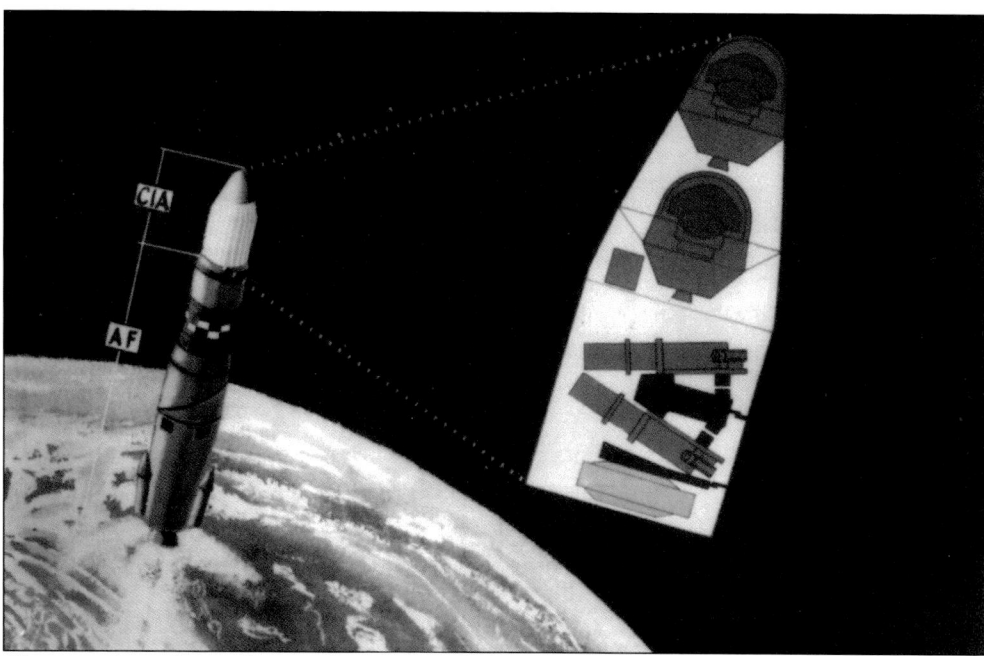

This artist's rendering depicts the moment before separation from the Thorad booster by the Agena spacecraft, and the KH-4B Corona system payload. The image also illustrates the Air Force's contributions to the Corona program—the booster and the Agena spacecraft—and the CIA's contribution of the camera payload. (National Reconnaissance Office.)

This fully assembled KH-4A Corona system payload is prepped for prelaunch testing and checkout. Of note are the two panoramic cameras, which can be seen near the bottom of the stack. KH-4A missions were launched out of SLC-3W at South Base, in addition to the SLC-1 and SLC-2 complexes at North Vandenberg. (National Reconnaissance Office.)

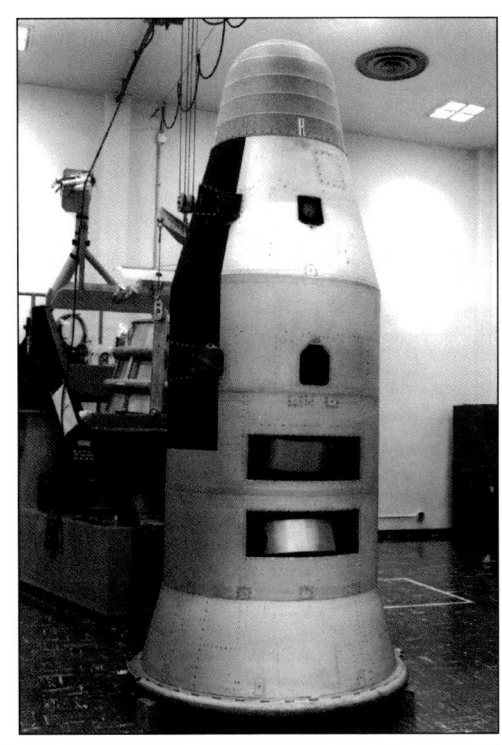

This image shows scale drawings of the three boosters used to launch the Corona satellite series. The Thor (left) launched the first generation of Corona (KH-1, KH-2, KH-3). The TAT, or Thrust Augmented Thor (center), launched the heavier KH-4 and two reentry capsules in the KH-4A satellite series. The Thorad (right) was an enhanced TAT and was used to launch the KH-4B's dual integrated stellar index camera (DISIC) and two film buckets. (National Reconnaissance Office.)

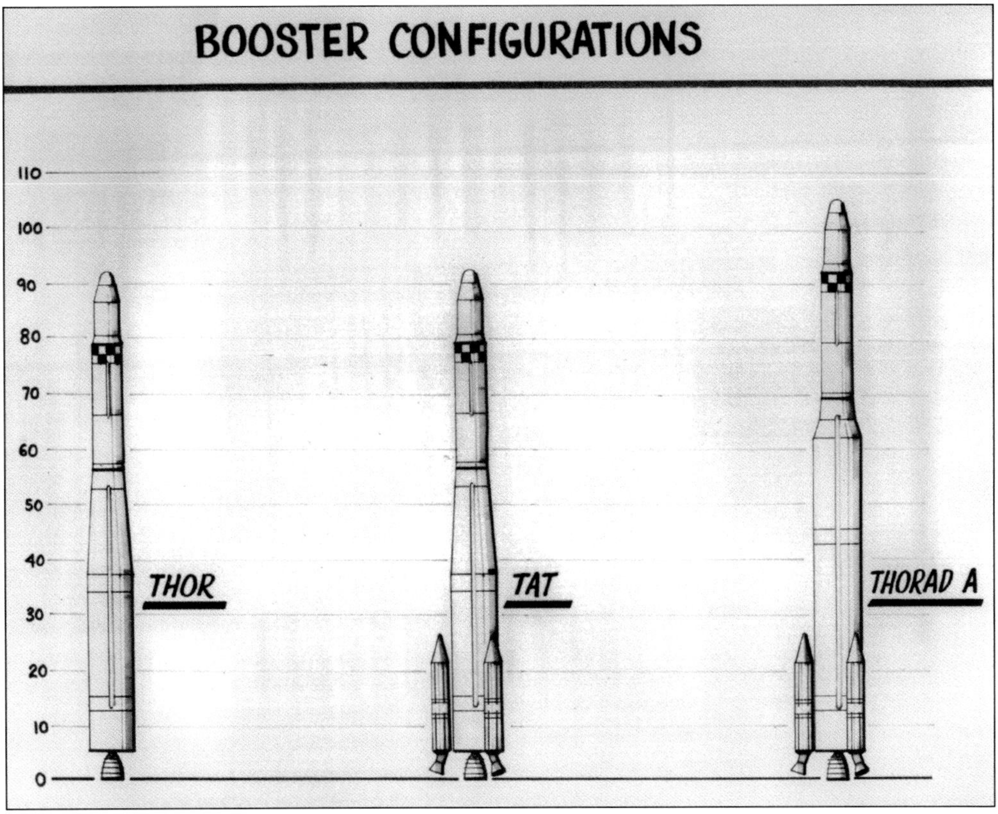

This map shows the location of Vandenberg, from which the Corona missions were launched. The southerly direction of the polar orbit was critical to maximizing coverage of the Soviet Union. The location was ideal for polar orbits because the launch vector offered the best possible downrange safety potential. (National Reconnaissance Office.)

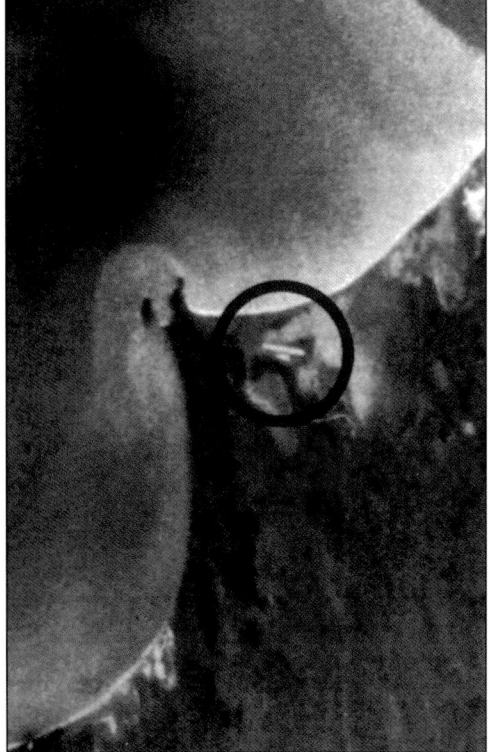

This is the first image taken by a Corona reconnaissance satellite, showing the Soviet Long Range Aviation airbase at Mys Shmidta (the runway is visible). Resolution from the first Corona (C) cameras was around 40 feet. A rating system called the National Imagery Interpretability Rating Scale (NIIRS) was developed by the American intelligence community to quantify the usefulness of imagery. This image represents NIIRS 1, the lowest end of usability. (National Reconnaissance Office.)

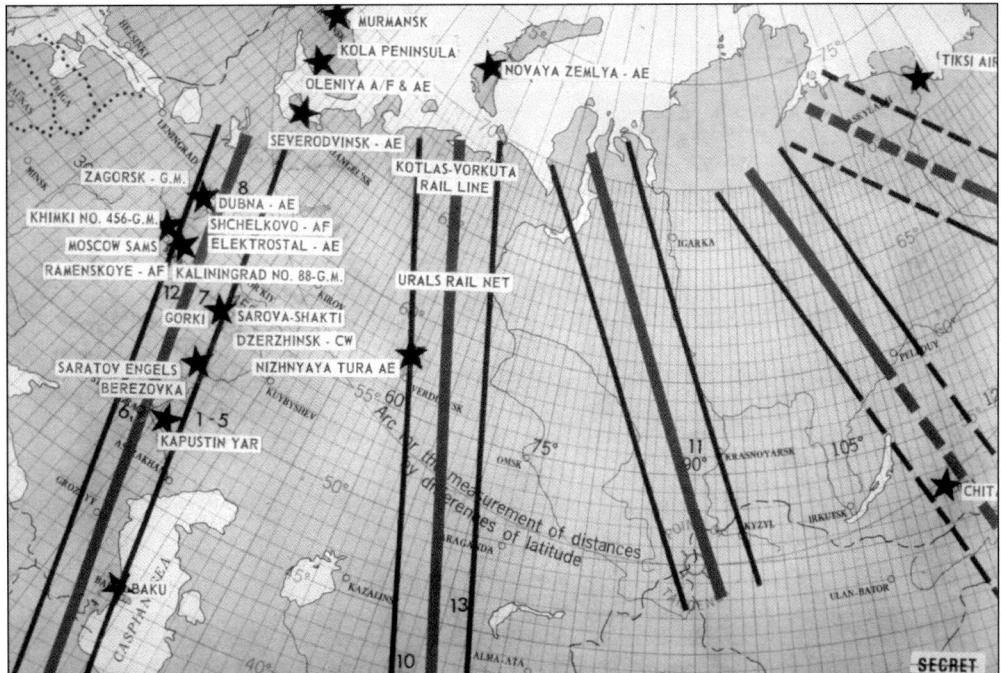

This orbit plot for an unidentified Corona mission over the USSR shows key targets (marked with stars). The thick middle line represents the orbital path of the spacecraft, while the two outer lines represent maximum extent of coverage on either side of the path. Early missions would have few orbital coverage paths like this, while later KH-4B missions—with two film buckets—could cover much of the Soviet landmass. (National Reconnaissance Office.)

According to Maj. Gen. John L. Martin, the NRO emblem began as a quasi-official seal that appeared on a "space reconnaissance academy certificate" that was awarded to NRO director Brockway McMillan on the occasion of his farewell party in September 1965. The image of a satellite circling a globe would persist throughout the decades. After the NRO's declassification in 1992, the US Army Institute of Heraldry formally recognized the logo. (National Reconnaissance Office.)

Here, Pres. John F. Kennedy inspects a reentry vehicle from a Discoverer/Corona vehicle at Vandenberg. While campaigning for the presidency, Kennedy used "missile gap" rhetoric to claim that the Soviets were ahead of the United States in ICBM development. After the 1960 election, President Kennedy was informed that a gap did indeed exist, but that it was heavily in favor of the United States. In January 1961, Corona imagery could not find a single operational Soviet ICBM site. (National Reconnaissance Office.)

Col. Charles "Moose" Mathison (third from left, in flight suit) presents *Discoverer XIII*'s film bucket to Lt. Gen. Bernard Schriever (left) and Gen. Thomas D. White (center). Mathison was vice commander of the 6594th Test Wing but was not cleared for Corona. He retrieved what he believed was a Discoverer capsule and transported it to Andrews AFB, in Maryland. Fortunately, there was no security compromise, as the "Lucky Thirteen" capsule contained no film. (National Reconnaissance Office.)

A White House publicity photograph from August 1960 shows Pres. Eisenhower (left) displaying the contents of the *Discoverer XIII* capsule—a folded American flag. Next to Eisenhower are USAF Chief of Staff Thomas White (center) and Col. "Moose" Mathison (right). The capsule was the first object to return to earth from space, beating the Soviet Union to the feat by nine days. (National Reconnaissance Office.)

The first KH-7 Gambit rides aloft on an Atlas-Agena rocket on July 12, 1963. The foundation was laid for the Gambit program before Corona had even tasted success. For the project, Eastman Kodak submitted a proposal for a 77-inch camera system—nicknamed "Sunset Strip." CIA director John McCone had suggested the Atlas-Agena booster for Corona due to a series of launch failures, but all available launchers were destined for Gambit or NASA. (National Reconnaissance Office.)

The first KH-8 Gambit-3 was launched at SLC-4W on a Titan IIIB/Agena-D stack, on July 29, 1966. The success of the Thor/Agena series allowed Agena developers to try different boost vehicles. Aside from the Corona series, the Agena filled the satellite bus role for the KH-5 Argon mapping camera, KH-6 Lanyard high-resolution camera, the Quill synthetic aperture radar payload, and the KH-7 and KH-8 Gambit series. (National Reconnaissance Office.)

Brig. Gen. William "Bill" King Jr. was the NRO's Program A director from August 1969 through March 1971—leading the efforts of the Corona, Gambit, and Hexagon satellite programs. Gen. King joined the NRO Office of Special Projects in 1961 and served as commander of the Air Force Satellite Control Facility (the "Blue Cube") in Sunnyvale, California, prior to his directorial assignment. Today, Vandenberg's heritage center holds many of General King's personal artifacts.

On July 28, 2010, the Air Force closed Onizuka Air Force Base in Sunnyvale. Satellite control functions were moved to the Ellison Onizuka Satellite Operations Facility at Vandenberg. The iconic Blue Cube (seen here) was built in the early 1960s to support the Discoverer/Corona program, and also supported Hexagon, Gambit, and other Department of Defense space activities.

Declared operational on January 4, 1959, Vandenberg Tracking Station was originally built to support the Discoverer/CORONA program. The station was part of the 6594th Test Wing (Satellite), controlled by the Air Force Satellite Control Facility "Blue Cube" in Sunnyvale. The station's callsign is COOK, representing the base's short-lived designation as Cooke Air Force Base.

This photograph of the US Capitol was taken by KH-7 Gambit-1 (Mission 4025) on February 19, 1966. Individual cars are visible in the parking lots and streets. High resolution images such as this provided ample work for imagery interpreters at the National Photographic Interpretation Center in Washington, DC. Corona (and later, Hexagon) missions would provide tipping for locations that needed higher resolution photographs, precipitating Gambit mission coverage. (National Reconnaissance Office.)

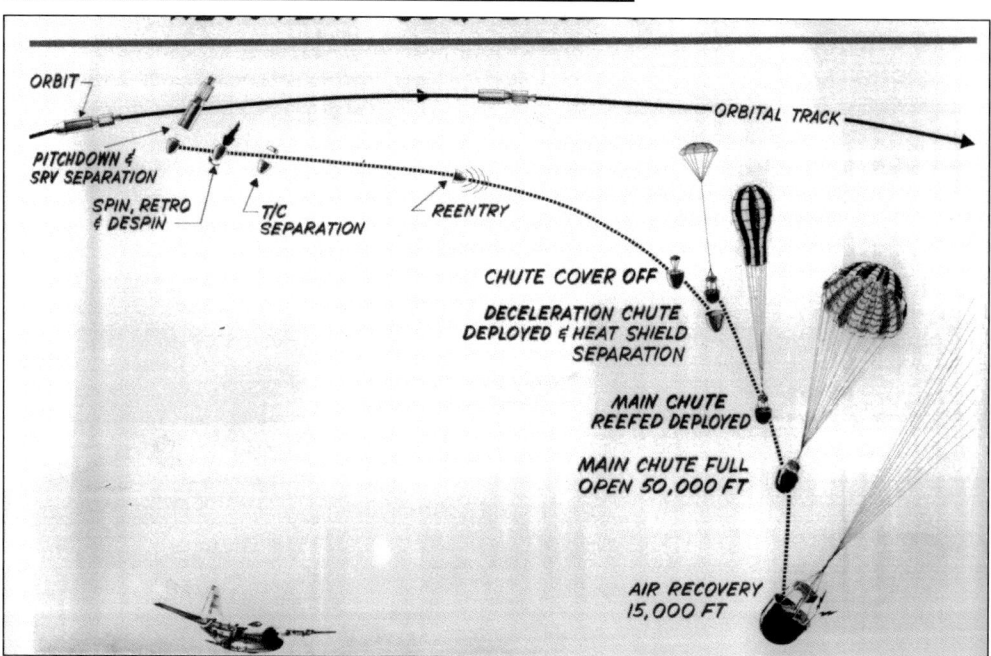

This diagram illustrates the aerial recovery process for all film-based photographic satellite system reentry vehicles (RVs). Aside from changes in the weight of the reentry vehicle, and the specific aircraft used, such as JC-119 or JC-130, the procedure stayed largely the same throughout the Corona, Gambit, and Hexagon programs. (National Reconnaissance Office.)

Launched on April 27, 1964, Corona Mission 1005 provided, as one wry NRO official put it, "valuable engineering data on non-optimum reentry survivability." After a successful start to the flight, the KI I-4A satellite started failing, prompting controllers to eject the film buckets over the Pacific in late May. It wasn't until July 1964 that two Venezuelan farm workers would stumble upon the wreckage and report it to the Venezuelan government. (National Reconnaissance Office.)

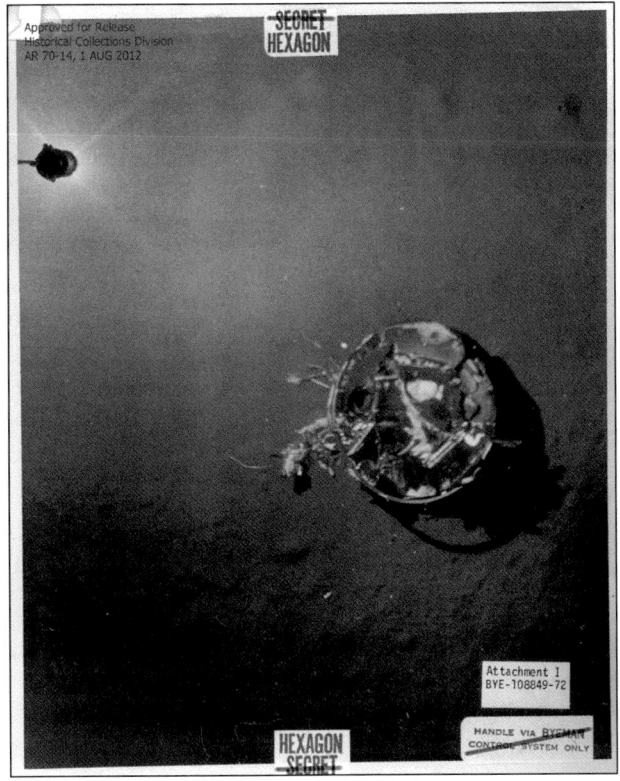

The remains of the first KH-9 Hexagon (Mission 1201-3) reside at a depth of 16,400 feet under the Pacific Ocean. During aerial recovery, the parachute on RV No. 3 was destroyed, and the capsule sank on impact. The CIA and Navy planned an eight-month recovery effort, which was executed on April 26, 1972. At the time, it was the deepest underwater salvage attempt ever made. The attempt failed, as the film disintegrated when the recovery vehicle ascended from the ocean floor. (Central Intelligence Agency.)

On April 18, 1986, the final KH-9 Hexagon (Mission 1220) was launched from SLC-4E aboard a Titan 34D booster. An explosion occurred seconds after liftoff, and the command destruct signal was issued at approximately 10 seconds after liftoff. Debris from the rocket damaged vehicles and buildings at SLC-4E. Investigators scoured the hills of South Vandenberg, searching for ribbons of film and pieces of the—then still classified—satellite. This tragedy brought an unceremonious end to US film-based satellite reconnaissance efforts, which had begun 27 years earlier. (Central Intelligence Agency.)

Shown here being lifted in a high-bay, the KH-9 Hexagon satellite was a wide-area search replacement for Corona—designed to spot targets for the Gambit series satellites to shoot high-resolution images of. A declassified interview with Dr. Hans Mark (director of the NRO, 1977–1979), revealed that the space shuttle payload bay was determined by the size of the Hexagon. Although the shuttle never took a KH-9 into orbit, this interview confirmed a theory long held by some space enthusiasts. (National Reconnaissance Office.)

The last Hexagon was restored at Vandenberg prior to its 2011 declassification. At the time of its first launch, in June 1971, Hexagon was the largest satellite the NRO had ever attempted to boost into orbit. The satellite measured 10 feet across and 59 feet long, and weighed about 27,000 pounds. Hexagon's unprecedented size prompted a local California newspaper reporter covering the first launch to nickname the unacknowledged spacecraft "Big Bird." (National Reconnaissance Office.)

The last remaining KH-9 Hexagon went on display at the National Museum of the United States Air Force (NMUSAF) in Dayton, Ohio, on January 26, 2012. In preparation for declassification, the NRO flew the Big Bird from Vandenberg to Chantilly, Virginia, and placed it on display for a one-day-only gala event during the 50th anniversary of the NRO on September 17, 2011.

Prior to its declassification in 2011, this Gambit vehicle came "home" to Vandenberg for refurbishment in preparation for public display. From their first launches in 1963, the KH-7 and KH-8 Gambit satellites set the standard for imagery collection. The Gambit-3 (KH-8) contained over 12,000 feet of 9.5-inch-wide film, and 3,600 feet of 5-inch film—giving it a search potential of over 17-million square miles. (National Reconnaissance Office.)

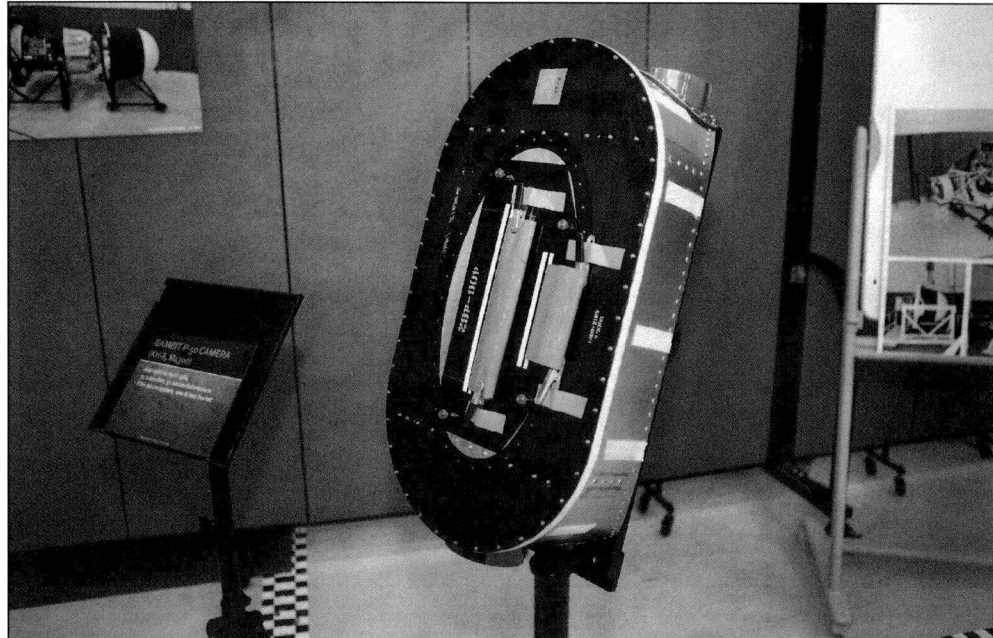

The Gambit-3 P-50 camera was on display at Vandenberg for a brief time following its declassification in 2011. The stated resolution in declassified documents for the Gambit camera was two to four feet ground resolved distance from an altitude of 500 miles. (National Reconnaissance Office.)

The last Gambit spacecraft sits within the NRO areas at Vandenberg. At the end of the Gambit program in 1984, Pres. Ronald Reagan wrote that "The technology of acquiring high quality pictures from space was perfected by the Gambit Program engineers; Gambit photographic clarity has yet to be surpassed. Through the years, intelligence gained from these photographs has been essential." (National Reconnaissance Office.)

A Gambit reentry vehicle sits on display at Vandenberg. The KH-7 featured a photographic resolution of 85 lines per millimeter, which translated to a ground resolution, at nadir, of about two feet. This resolution was considered good in 1961, when Gambit's development was initiated, and was still comparable to some of the best available commercial systems launched in the late 1990s and early 21st century, such as Quickbird and IKONOS. (National Reconnaissance Office.)

Another Gambit satellite is on display at the NMUSAF in Dayton, Ohio. Along with a Hexagon, a KH-7 Gambit-1 and KH-8 Gambit-3 were placed on display at the NMUSAF—completing the picture of national space reconnaissance through the mid-1980s. It may be another few decades before the museum will be able to tell the tales of today's high-flying spies.

The logo of NRO Vandenberg displays elements specific to its West Coast home, such as the mountain lion common to Vandenberg's lands. The first publicly acknowledged NRO satellite launch took place at Vandenberg in December 1996 on a Titan IV rocket. Prior to December 1996, the NRO did not acknowledge its launches—even after its 1992 declassification. (National Reconnaissance Office.)

The logo of NROL-39 displays an octopus encompassing the world, with the phrase, "Nothing is beyond our reach." "Patch-ology," a semi-humorous reference to the study of NRO patches, has become an active part of amateur satellite observer websites and blogs. (National Reconnaissance Office.)

The first West Coast Delta IV Heavy Launch Vehicle was launched from SLC-6 on January 20, 2011, carrying a national security payload for the NRO. On October 1, 1978, Pres. Jimmy Carter stated that "Photoreconnaissance satellites have become an important stabilizing factor in world affairs in the monitoring of arms control agreements. They make immense contribution to the security of all nations." Through the decades, Vandenberg personnel—civilians, contractors and military—made tremendous contributions to the National Reconnaissance Program and continue to do so today.

Four

DAWN OF A NEW ERA (1977–1989)

The beginning of the 1980s brought a host of changes to Vandenberg. The election of Pres. Ronald Reagan changed the direction of the nation from relative passivity in the mid-1970s to an active approach in many matters foreign and domestic. Reagan's National Security Decision Directive-12, titled "Strategic Forces Modernization Program," guided the long-term development of strategic forces including the MX (later renamed LGM-118A Peacekeeper) ICBM basing modes in refurbished Minuteman III units, as well as the retirement of the LGM-25C Titan II ICBM.

Changes to the civilian space program also brought the promise of a financial boon to the local economy. Vandenberg had been identified as a shuttle launch site as early as 1972, with the mothballed SLC-6 site marked as the primary candidate location. Construction on shuttle facilities began in 1979 and continued throughout the early part of the 1980s. The loss of the space shuttle *Challenger* on January 28, 1986, during its 25th mission, made the Air Force and NASA re-examine the need for a West Coast launch site. In late 1986, SLC-6 was reduced to "operational caretaker status," and was finally eliminated as a shuttle launch site in 1988.

The Honda Canyon fire of December 20, 1977, would take the lives of four individuals: the base commander, Col. Joseph Turner; Fire Chief Billy Bell; Assistant Fire Chief Eugene Cooper; and Clarence McCauley, a heavy equipment operator. (Joe Valencia.)

Flames from the Honda Canyon fire are seen from Coast Road. The volatility and unpredictable nature of the fire was reinforced many times throughout the two-day ordeal. No lesson was more harrowing than the loss of human life. Between 8:56 a.m. and 2:30 p.m. on December 20, 1977, the flames overran fire and police crews eight times and damaged many vehicles. (Marshall Goddard.)

Two unidentified men talk about response plans as the fire rages in the background. The Honda Canyon fire left an indelible mark on the history of Vandenberg. The loss of human life, along with the devastation upon the landscape, led to a stronger partnership between Santa Barbara County firefighters and Vandenberg fire crews. This relationship served the base and county well in the 2009 and 2014 fires on Vandenberg. (Joe Valencia.)

Gen. David Gray (at right), 1st Strategic Aerospace Division commander, inspects the situation on South Vandenberg with Lt. Col. Edward Johnson, commander of Vandenberg's security police force. (Joe Valencia.)

The vehicle containing Santa Barbara battalion chief Don Perry, hotshot crew superintendent Joe Lindaman, and firefighters Grant Gabbert and John Grossini is pictured here. The four survived a fire burnover when their vehicle got stuck and was overtaken by flames. (Joe Valencia.)

This Vandenberg Launch and Landing Site patch depicts the polar orbit path near the center of the Air Force's standard shield logo. Vandenberg was intended to be a self-contained location to prepare, launch, land, and transport the space shuttle without relying on Cape Canaveral's facilities, equipment, or personnel. There were even plans to have two shuttles permanently stationed in California.

An early artist's concept shows a shuttle launch from SLC-6, with the Mobile Service Tower (MST) in the background. Refurbishment of the MOL facilities, and the construction of new buildings, cost about $4 billion. The construction used roughly 250,000 cubic yards of concrete (equivalent to a 25-mile, four-lane interstate highway), 9,000 tons of reinforcing steel, and 15,000 tons of structural steel.

This aerial view of the SLC-6 shows structures including, from the left, the payload preparation facility and mobile payload change-out facility (side-by-side, with white stripe mid-height); the mobile shuttle assembly building (with "USAF" on the side); the space shuttle "stack," with its access tower partially hidden; and the mobile service tower. Below the access tower and pad are two triangular concrete ducts, which vented the rocket exhaust away from the pad.

This illustration provides an example of the shuttle's lift capacity from the program's early years. The Greyhound Bus was a thinly veiled comparison to the KH-9 Hexagon satellite. The dimensions of the cargo bay included a 15-foot diameter and a 60-foot length, corresponding to Hexagon's 10-foot diameter and 60-foot length. Bureaucratic battles between NASA and the NRO, and the 1986 *Challenger* explosion, kept Hexagon off the shuttle manifest.

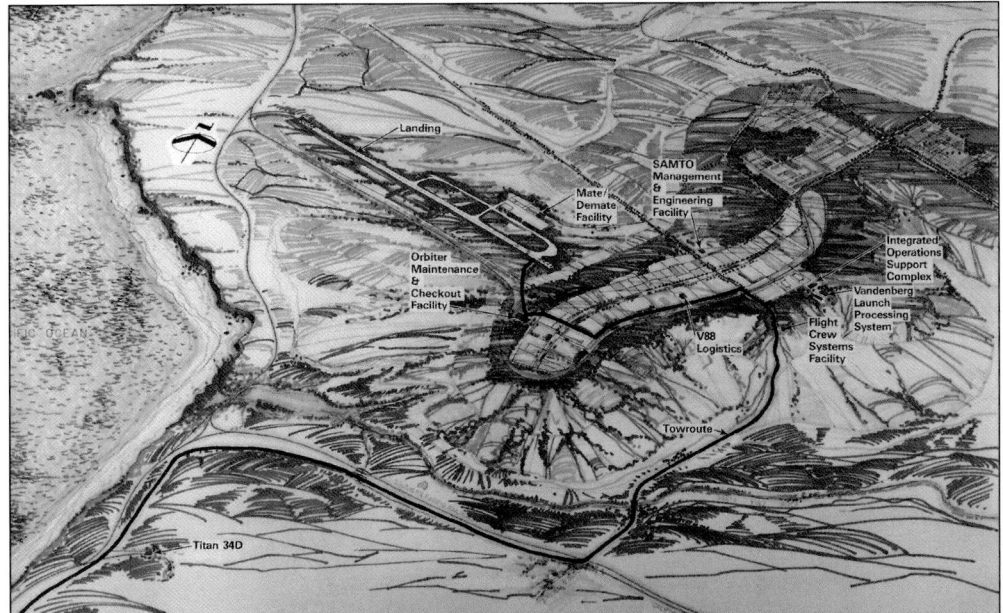

The North Vandenberg shuttle facilities included a three-mile runway with a mate/demate facility, a maintenance and checkout facility, and an operations support complex that housed the launch processing system and flight crew systems facility. The dark line on this map displays the "tow route," along which the shuttle would travel for launching at SLC-6. Many of these facilities have been repurposed, while others have been stripped of their equipment in the intervening decades.

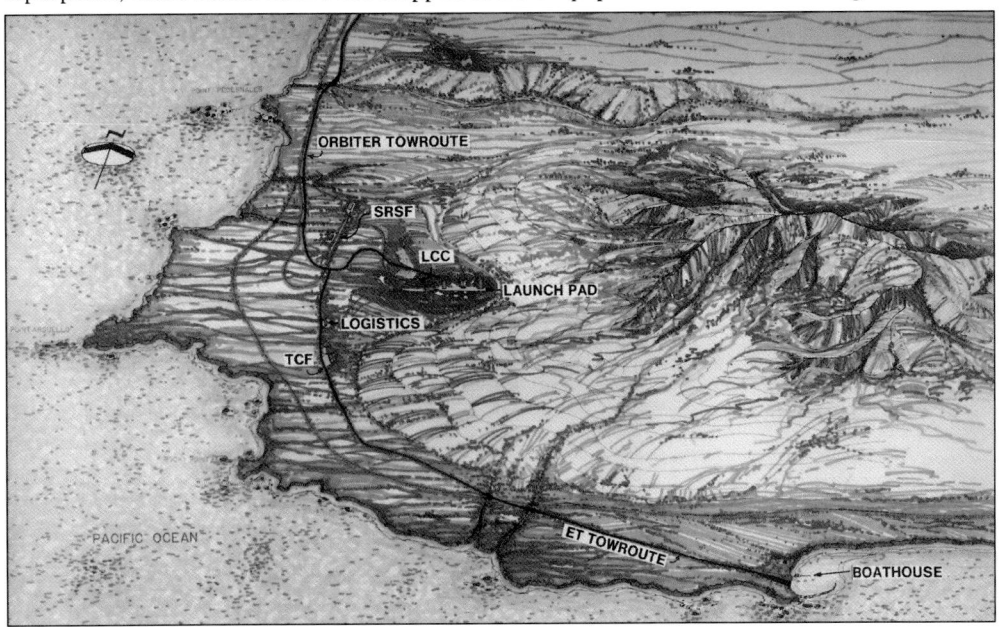

The South Vandenberg facilities contained the nexus of shuttle operations: SLC-6. The orbiter would travel along the tow route, while the solid-rocket boosters and external tank would arrive at the Boathouse from Port Hueneme—and then travel on their own tow route to SLC-6. The southern naval facility (not pictured) would house the two SRB retrieval boats that combed the ocean for the rocket boosters.

Here, the OV-101 *Enterprise* sits atop an Orbiter Transportation System vehicle, for travel down to South Vandenberg. This 76-wheel vehicle allows horizontal conveyance of the shuttle along the 15-mile route to SLC-6. A recent online government auction for discarded shuttle support equipment saw this transport sell for $37,000—a fraction of its original purchase cost. Also of note are the white wisps at the top of the photograph, which are typical of Vandenberg's fog.

On January 28, 1985, the *Enterprise* made its long journey along 13th Street, toward South Vandenberg. Telephone poles were set away from the road, and signs were either shortened or had a lowering hinge. Along the downward route, the shale was cut away to provide a minimum two-foot clearance for the shuttle's wings. Personnel (seen at left and right, on the slope cutout) monitored the wing clearance during travel.

Here, the *Enterprise* approaches SLC-6, with the Shuttle Assembly Building shrouded in typical Vandenberg fog. Exactly one year later, on January 28, 1986, the explosion of the shuttle *Challenger* would derail the manned spaceflight program and push back the first Vandenberg flight until 1992. In January 1987, SLC-6 was placed on "minimum facility standby," with the launch put on indefinite hold. April 1988 saw the complex reduced to caretaker status, reducing maintenance costs.

The Orbiter Transportation System reaches its destination—the Shuttle Assembly Building. The tracks allowed the SAB and mobile service tower to move towards each other and completely enclose the launch pad. Prior to launch, the buildings would move approximately 300 feet back from the pad. The size of the buildings allowed them to travel no faster than 40 feet per minute, after being lifted nine inches off the ground by 72 hydraulic jacks.

The Space Transportation System's external tank (ET) arrives at the boat dock. ETs would travel from Mississippi, through the Panama Canal, to Port Hueneme south of Vandenberg. These additional shuttle facilities would also contain berthing for the solid rocket booster retrieval ships. A processing facility for the tanks stood outside of the SLC-6 complex, allowing for the storage of four tanks, with a fifth being processed.

Inside the Shuttle Assembly Building (SAB), the orbiter is lifted for mating to the external tank and two solid rocket boosters. The SAB was 220 feet high and weighed over 4,670 tons. It was designed to protect the shuttle from the elements during processing operations, and contained one of the two cranes required to lift the shuttle and external tanks into an upright position.

One of the possible patch designs for the cancelled STS-62A mission showed the polar orbiting path that was possible from California, and featured the identifier "V1," to commemorate Vandenberg's first shuttle launch. (Timothy Gagnon.)

The Teal Ruby satellite is on display within this Shuttle Simulator cargo bay. Teal Ruby was an experimental satellite, designated as the first payload launched from Vandenberg aboard STS-62A. The satellite was designed to detect hostile missile launches, giving US military forces early warning of a nuclear attack. Since it never flew, Teal Ruby remained in storage until its unveiling at the National Museum of the US Air Force in Dayton, Ohio, in 2014. (Wayne McMurry.)

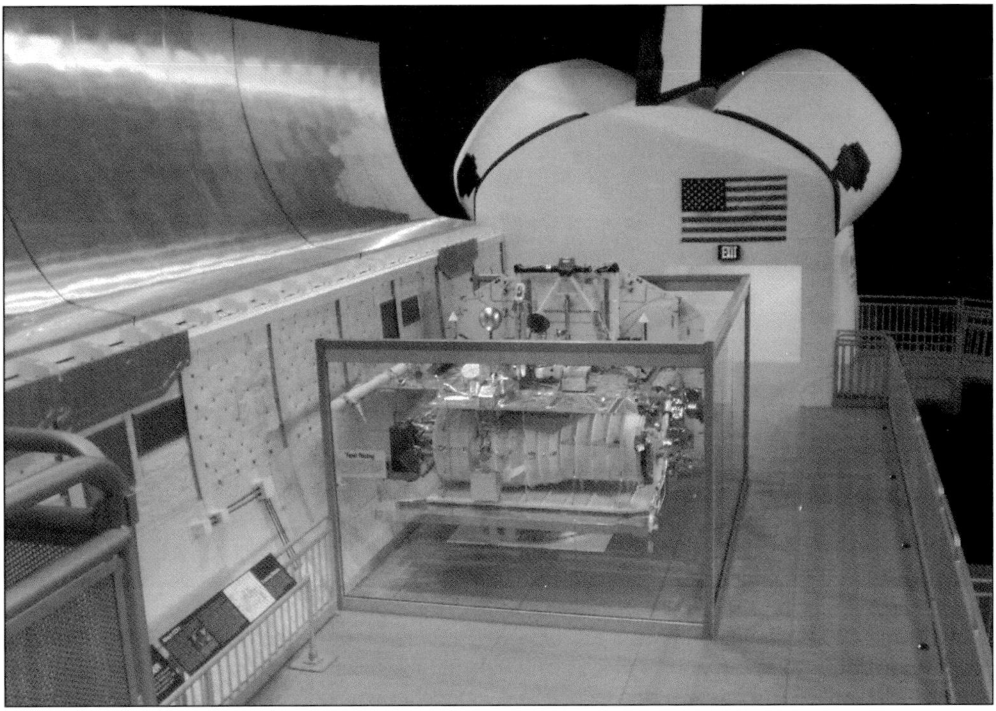

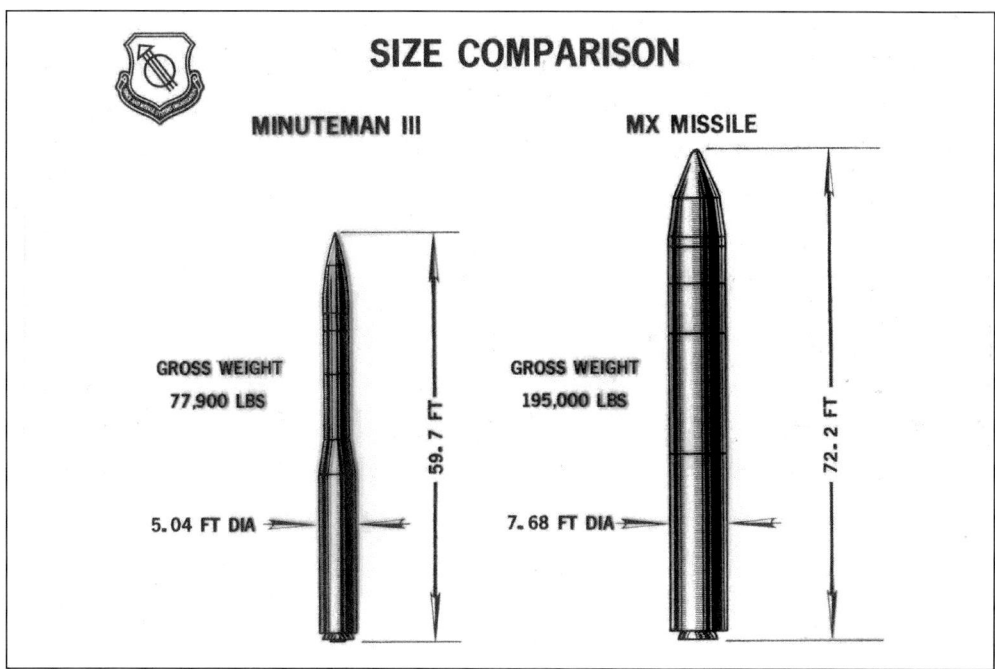

On this chart, the fourth-generation ICBM—designated here as "MX"—is compared to a third-generation Minuteman III. Modifications to Minuteman silos were required to hold the LGM-118A, designated the "Peacekeeper" by President Reagan. The first of 50 Peacekeepers went on alert at F.E. Warren Air Force Base on October 10, 1986. With changes in national security priorities, the entire force of Peacekeepers would be retired by September 19, 2005.

In this photograph, an LGM-118A Peacekeeper launches from LF-05, on North Vandenberg. Unlike Minuteman ICBM launches, the Peacekeeper's "exit" from the launch tube was relatively clean. The benefit of cold launch technology—ejection from the silo before stage one ignition—allowed the rapid reuse of the launch facility for a post-attack, second-strike capability. After the first salvo, SAC maintenance crews could "reload" a Peacekeeper silo with relative ease, unlike a scorching Minuteman launch.

This early test of the Peacekeeper featured a full missile fired out of an aboveground steam gas generator tube. For the aboveground tests, the launch tube erects the missile, while the launch eject gas generator ejects the missile prior to first stage ignition. The gas generator uses a solid propellant to vaporize water, forcing the steam pressure to "pop" the missile skyward.

The logo of the Peacekeeper Rail Garrison showcased the basing mode's selling point: survivability through mobility. On December 19, 1986, Pres. Ronald Reagan chose the program from seven options, believing that mobility would deter nuclear attack. The logic behind rail mobility was that "an aggressor's only recourse for a successful attack is a large barrage requiring substantial resources."

A mockup Peacekeeper Rail Garrison train sits inside of its "igloo" at Vandenberg Air Force Base during testing. The basic PKRG train consisted of two locomotives, a fuel car, a maintenance car, two security cars, two missile launch cars, and a launch control center (LCC) car. The LCC car held the missile combat crew and train commander. After the program's cancellation in 1991, the command and control console was given to Minuteman as Rapid Execution and Combat Targeting (REACT).

The Peacekeeper Rail Garrison train leaves its protective igloo during testing at Vandenberg. The Train Alert Shelters were earth-covered igloos, with a shed attached for supplemental train cars. The site also housed communications, electrical, and environmental control equipment for the train and crew. Ports in the roof of the TAS were able to open, which allowed missiles to be launched from within the garrison.

This CQM-10B Bomarc-B target drone, serial number 60-0909, was launched from Launch Complex BOM1 on May 1, 1977. Bomarc was originally created as a nuclear-tipped, long-range anti-aircraft missile. Early deployments of Bomarc were around the Eastern Seaboard and central Midwest. Maps of Vandenberg in the 1960s show a location earmarked for Bomarc installation, but the system was cancelled before construction began. After retirement, Bomarc drones were launched as Navy air-to-air targets.

A sign at Vandenberg greets Olympic Arena competitors and declares 1988 to be the "Year of the SAC Alert Force." In a memo outlining this event, CINCSAC general John T. Chain Jr. stated that "Those initial alert crews and support personnel formed the cornerstone of America's deterrence . . . [SAC personnel] should never forget that it is their vigilance and dedication which allow Americans to live in freedom in this great nation."

Three missile maintainers from the Malmstrom Air Force Base's 341st Strategic Missile Wing pose in front of their toolboxes during Olympic Arena 1988. In the years following Curtain Raiser, the missile competition came to include missile maintenance members and security forces as part of the events. Note the handles on the toolboxes, which are shaped to resemble miniature Minuteman missiles.

Capt. Sue Cox and 2nd Lt. Becky Estabrook took this crew snapshot for Olympic Arena public releases. A Minuteman crew consisting of two women was groundbreaking at the time, as official surveys from 1980 found that there was a negative reaction to mixed Minuteman and Peacekeeper crews from crewmembers and their spouses. Whiteman Air Force Base's 351st Strategic Missile Wing (SMW) was the first to integrate women into the Minuteman program. Captain Cox was previously a Titan crewmember, while Lieutenant Estabrook was fresh out of training.

In this photograph, 1st Lt. Sandra Ramos proudly displays the 341st SMW's "First Aces" garb during Olympic Arena 1988. Ramos would continue through a very successful career as a missile combat crewmember, and an expert in nuclear weapons. She eventually became the commander of the Nuclear Weapons Center at Kirtland Air Force Base, New Mexico.

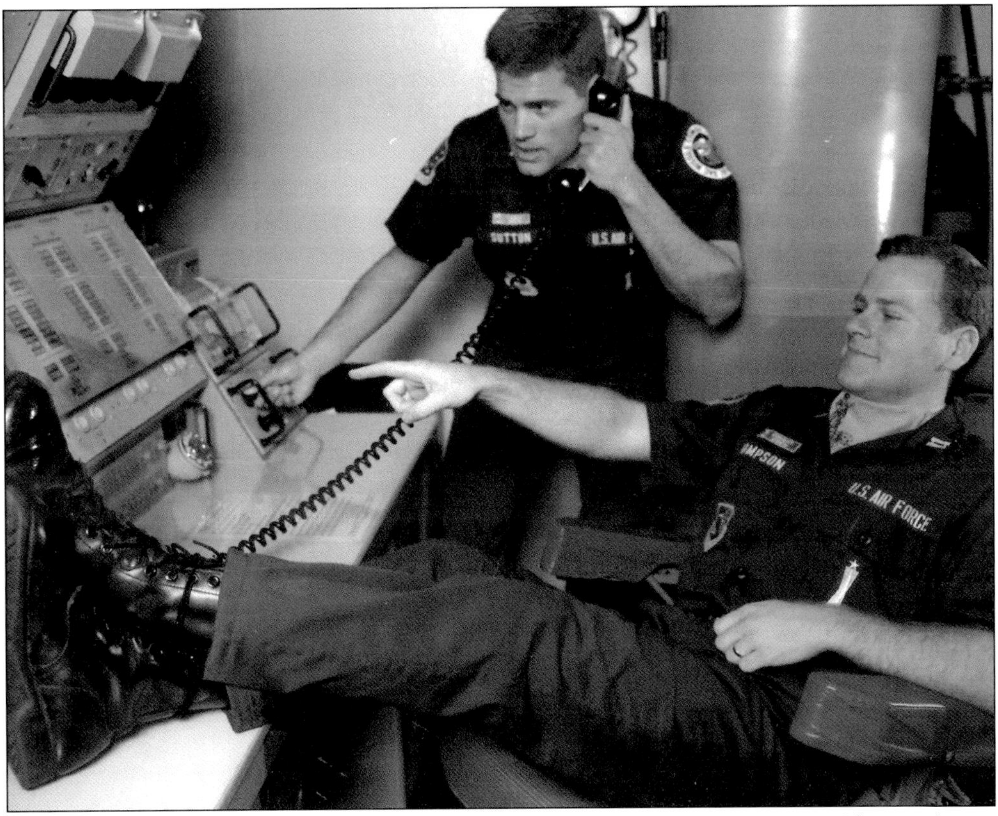

In a show of good humor, two missileers goof around during a photo opportunity at Olympic Arena. While it cannot be proven that missile combat crews work with their feet up on the command console, the deputy's (standing) worried look and commander's (sitting) relaxed pose raise the real question—if both crew members are at one console, who's minding the other one?

A decade before GPS became a household term, this Atlas E/F launched the fifth NAVSTAR GPS satellite into orbit on February 9, 1980, from SLC-3E. From 1978 to 1985, the first 11 GPS satellites (Block I) were launched from Vandenberg on Atlas E/F boosters with solid rocket upper stages. GPS technology at the time was rudimentary, requiring "portable" receivers that weighed over 20 pounds and were strapped to the back of an infantryman.

The final Atlas H launch took place on May 15, 1987, from SLC-3E. The payload was a national security satellite system for the Navy. It would be twelve and a half years before SLC-3E would see another rocket launch—an Atlas IIAS lifting a NASA earth observation satellite.

Five

BUSINESS AS USUAL (1990–PRESENT)

With the end of the Cold War, changes within the Air Force's internal structure sent ripples throughout its subordinate organizations. Most prevalent at Vandenberg was the deactivation of Strategic Air Command in 1992. For a brief period, all previously designated strategic assets, such as bombers and missiles, were assigned to Air Combat Command. This change did not last long, as Air Force Space Command took over the ICBM mission in 1993. Western Range testing and ICBM instruction remained with the experienced cadre at Vandenberg.

The rest of the 1990s saw national security payloads placed aloft by Vandenberg's skilled crews. Titan IV "heavy" launches, and the follow-on Evolved Expendable Launch Vehicles (Delta IV and Atlas V), would continue the record of success established in past decades. The retirement of the Titan family, with the last Titan IV launch in 2005, would see an end to the legacy of an outstanding family of rockets. The Delta IV and Atlas V, while not direct descendants of the Thor IRBM and Atlas ICBM, continue their rocket family's name and reputation for success in mission accomplishment.

After the events of September 11, 2001, Vandenberg would see its first combat casualty in the global war on terror. Sr. Amn. Daniel Johnson, an explosive ordnance disposal technician, lost his life disarming an improvised explosive device in Afghanistan. The Vandenberg family paid respectful tribute to Sr. Amn. Johnson's family and surviving widow with a memorial ceremony and dedication.

In the late 2000s, more changes saw the ICBM mission moved from Air Force Space Command to the "new" Air Force Global Strike Command—itself a reinvigorated version of Strategic Air Command. Even with the new command, ICBM operations continue to be an integral part of Team Vandenberg.

The Western Space and Missile Center was the organization responsible for the Western Test Range, which stretched from the California coast to the South Pacific Ocean. In 1991, a shift of organizations throughout the Air Force saw Air Force Space Command re-designate the WSMC as the 30th Space Wing.

Two security forces members guard Vandenberg's main gate during the 1990 Olympic Arena competition. In later years, this structure would be torn down and replaced with infrastructure increasing force protection.

Members of the 341st Strategic Missile Wing—the overall winners of the 1991 Olympic Arena competition—pose on stage during the trophy presentation. The following 12 months would see drastic changes for America's nuclear forces. On September 28, 1991, Pres. George H.W. Bush issued orders to take all Minuteman II missiles off alert and cease airborne alerts for B-52 crews. The end of the Cold War was nigh.

The 1992 Olympic Arena competition saw the 44th Missile Wing's "Black Hills Bandits" win the Blanchard Trophy for best missile wing. Changes for America's strategic forces were already afoot when the competition took place. Missile and bombardment wings dropped the "Strategic" from their designations, and—soon after—Strategic Air Command would be deactivated as part of an Air Force effort to eliminate the "tactical" and "strategic" descriptors.

In 2008, Vandenberg refurbished the Honda Ridge rock art–viewing platform. Following consultation with the Chumash, the platform was upgraded—enhancing and protecting the setting of the sacred site, while making it safer for visitors. Additions included a guest register, an interpretive panel, and a pamphlet dispenser at the trailhead. This, and many other similar efforts, earned Vandenberg the title of most outstanding cultural resources management program in the Air Force. (Page Family, CA Chapter.)

Demolition crews collapsed part of the SLC-4E mobile service tower on August 2, 2011. The first launches from SLC-4E were Atlas-Agena boosters, carrying KH-7 Gambit satellites. Later, the pad was refurbished to launch Titans, including Titan IIIDs carrying KH-9 Hexagon, Titan 34Ds lifting KH-9s, and other national security payloads. The final Titan variant at SLC-4E was the Titan IV heavy lift booster, with the capacity to lift 47,000 pounds into low earth orbit.

A fish-eye lens photograph of a Minuteman Launch Control Center shows the Rapid Execution and Combat Targeting (REACT) console. Upgrades to the nuclear command and control system began in the 1980s under President Reagan. REACT was originally developed for the Peacekeeper Rail Garrison, and the console was designed to fit in a rail car. After the Rail Garrison program was cancelled, REACT was adapted for the Minuteman system. (National Park Service.)

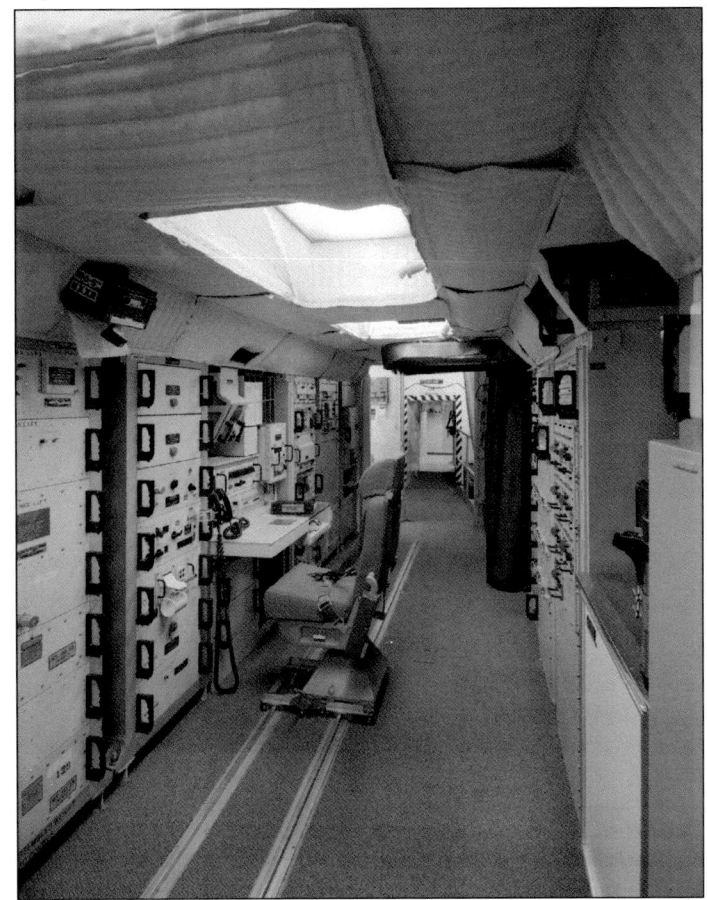

This shot of a Launch Control Center shows the sterile environment that missile combat crewmembers work in. Five LCCs were built on Vandenberg during the tenure of the Minuteman program, reflecting various configurations. One resides underwater, due to the rising water table, while another was deemed biologically unsafe due to mold contaminants, and was filled with rock debris. Others exist in various states of disrepair. Active LCCs still exist, however, to assist in Minuteman Follow-on Test & Evaluation launches. (National Park Service.)

These cylindrical steel structures hold the Minuteman ICBM while it is in the launch facility. After the missile's first stage ignites, it slips up and out of the launch tube. After launch, these support frames are refurbished and used again during subsequent launches.

Airmen from the 576th Flight Test Squadron's missile handling team install a cable raceway on a Minuteman III on February 3, 2014. This team transports ICBMs to their North Vandenberg launch facilities and performs operational checks of the flight safety destruct ordnance package on the boosters. Because it is based underground, the missile has been treated with a fungicide, lending it a green color. No operational missile is painted white.

S.Sgt. Kade McMurry, at left, stands on the operations floor of the Joint Space Operations Center (JSpOC). The JSpOC provides operational employment of worldwide joint space forces and enables the US military to integrate space power into global military operations. It also performs screenings on approximately 1,100 active satellites daily, mitigating the danger of these systems colliding with the more than 22,000 trackable objects orbiting the Earth.

M.Sgt. Michael Roberts, a sensor management analyst from the JSpOC, verifies the accuracy of a radar tracking station's observations—focused on several man-made objects floating in space. Sgt. Roberts was also a minor celebrity on Vandenberg, as he starred in an Air Force recruiting commercial. After a dramatized collision in space, Roberts informed the crew that harmful debris was "twenty kilometers and closing" toward an American satellite.

Lt. Gen. Susan J. Helms, commander of the Joint Functional Component Command for Space speaks to a group of airmen at Vandenberg. In addition to being the highest-ranking military officer on base, Gen. Helms was also the top space officer for US Strategic Command. She is known for holding the world record for the single longest extra-vehicular activity (spacewalk) as well as being the first female military astronaut.

In early October 2009, a fire at Vandenberg torched 617 acres near the Pine Canyon area. The fire was started by downed power lines, but was contained after a week due to the efforts of fire fighters from the base and around Santa Barbara County.

Sr. Amn. Daniel Johnson, a 23-year-old Illinois native, was killed on October 5, 2010, in Kandahar, Afghanistan. After enlisting in the Air Force in November 2006, Johnson chose the Explosive Ordnance Disposal career field. In October 2007, he was assigned to Vandenberg's 30th Civil Engineer Squadron. A veteran of Iraq and Afghanistan, Johnson helped disarm improvised explosive devices that threatened civilians and coalition forces.

On November 11, 2011, a memorial on California Boulevard was dedicated to Sr. Amn. Daniel Johnson. This stone memorial resides on the "Missile V" junction. Johnson's widow, Kristen Johnson, spoke at the ceremony, along with his colleagues and commander. The end of the memorial service culminated in a roll call for the EOD team members, marked by a poignant silence after Johnson's name was called with no following reply.

In this photograph, 30th Security Forces Squadron members drill for Police Week 2014, under the watchful eye of unit trainer T.Sgt. Carmine Androsiglio (in uniform). Pres. John F. Kennedy signed a proclamation in 1962 designating May 15 as Peace Officers Memorial Day, and its corresponding week as Police Week. Events included a 24-hour vigilant guard, and the reading of names of 120 peace officers killed in the line of duty. (Page Family, CA Chapter.)

S.Sgt. Andrea Lewis, 30th Security Forces Squadron member, says goodbye to her horse, Willie, during his official retirement ceremony. Since 1999, Vandenberg has been the only Air Force base with a mounted horse unit for use in search and rescue operations and patrols into rough terrain. After retirement, Willie was sent to the Jack Auchterlonie Memorial Equine Sanctuary in Twentynine Palms, California.

The remnants of a boat remain on Minuteman Beach after an accident on November 24, 2009. Vandenberg's emergency responders rescued one injured survivor from the boating accident off the coast. (Page Family, CA Chapter.)

As a "fit to fight" force, the units on Vandenberg take advantage of their ample opportunities to perform physical training on the beaches. (Page Family, CA Chapter.)

The Boathouse on South Vandenberg overlooks the ocean and the entry to the Santa Barbara Channel. The location is a popular venue on the base, hosting events that range from wine tastings to celebratory unit barbeques. The house is regularly kept up by base personnel, who paint, do minor carpentry, and handle general cleanup. (Page Family, CA Chapter.)

Capt. Phillip Mudakha (left) and other members of the Joint Space Operations Center fish off the boat dock on South Vandenberg. Members of the Vandenberg Dive Club, the Aqualliers, are stewards of the Boathouse dock area. The club routinely camps at the Boathouse, fishes, and dives in the waters off the dock.

A 533rd Training Squadron class poses at an entry sign proudly proclaiming "Welcome to (Counter) Space Country." The training units on base provide qualification training for space surveillance, missile warning, spacelift, and satellite command and control operators.

Next generation Air Force warriors pose at the Ronald Reagan Memorial Observation Site on North Base. Class pictures such as this are a common sight inside the various classrooms in Vandenberg's training schoolhouse. While most class photographs are mundane, others have pushed the boundaries of wackiness, legality, and common sense.

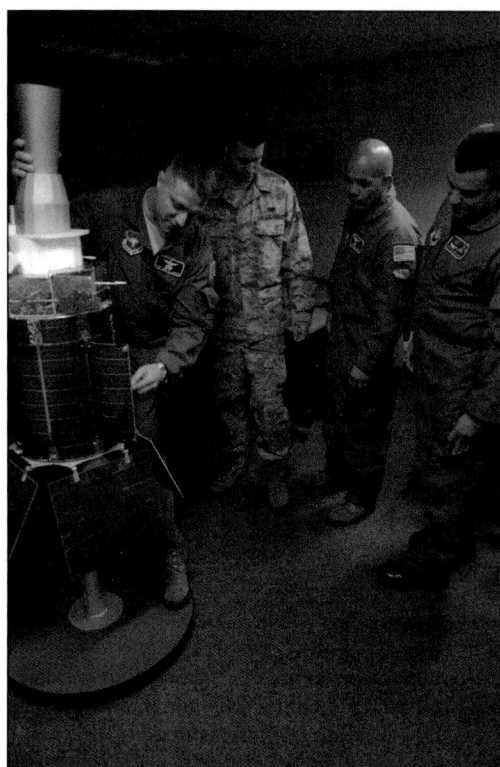

S.Sgt. Danial St. James (left), a 533rd Training Squadron space based infrared systems instructor, explains the sub systems of Defense Support Program satellites to students. The 533rd TRS provides initial qualification training for attack warning, space surveillance, and satellite command and control missions.

Trainees celebrate Thanksgiving at the 381st Training Group dining facilities. Gatherings such as this allow the Air Force family to support its newest members when they are separated from loved ones during the holidays.

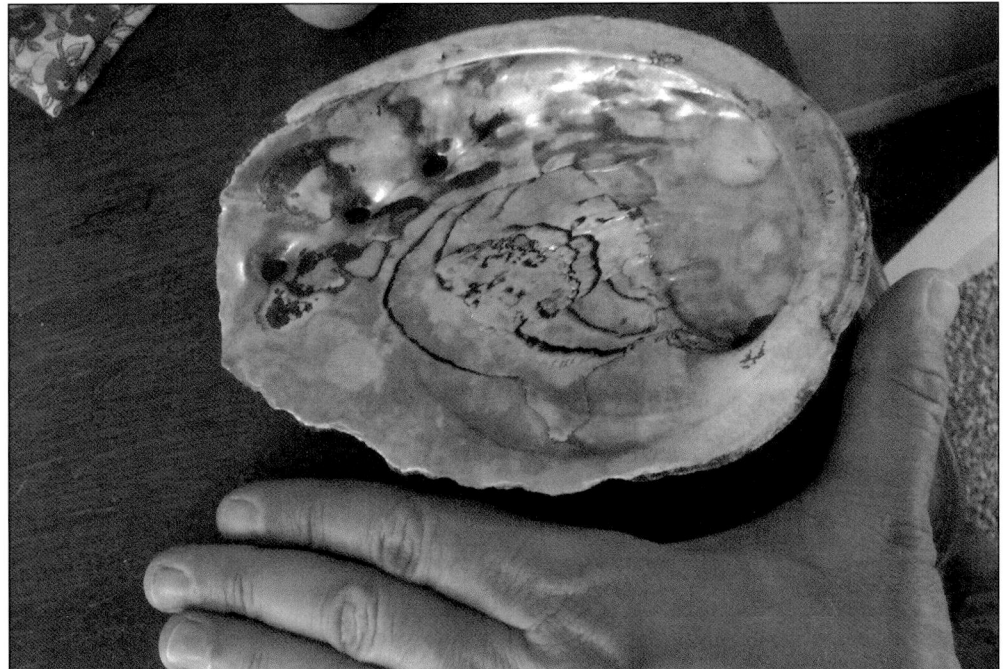

This red abalone shell (*Haliotis rufescens*) represents one of the seven species of abalone found off the California coast. Abalone populations experienced severe declines from the 1960s to 1990s. Abalone shells, either whole (such as this one) or in pieces, can be found after high tides on Vandenberg's beaches. (Page Family, CA Chapter.)

Coyotes (*Canis latrans*) often wander the grounds of Vandenberg. Bobcats, foxes, and mountain lions have also been spotted on the grounds. (Page Family, CA Chapter.)

A California mule deer (*Odocoileus hemionus*, subspecies *californicus*) runs through the brush at Vandenberg's Cocheo Park. For Vandenberg service-people and their families, wildlife is a common sight within the garrison and housing areas. (Page Family, CA Chapter.)

In this photograph, a peregrine falcon perches on a fence post on North Vandenberg. Over 344 species of bird can be found on base property. The base maintains a strong wildlife conservation force to protect the base's varied habitats, including wetlands, riparian woodlands, coastal beaches and dunes, rocky shoreline, burton mesa chaparral, coastal sage and dune scrub, oak woodland, grassland, tanbark oak woodland, and bishop pine forest. (Page Family, CA Chapter.)

Here, Joint Space Operations Center personnel, led by Col. John Wagner (front row, right), pose in their high bay, which was formerly used to prepare Titan II and IV boosters. JSpOC tasks the Space Surveillance Network (SSN)—a worldwide network of 30 space surveillance sensors—to observe orbital objects. The crews match sensor observations to the orbiting objects and maintain the Satellite Catalog, a comprehensive listing of all trackable objects in space.

Members of Task Force Minot pose in front of the 576th Flight Test Squadron. These personnel represent only a fraction of the people who make these test launches a success. From the rocket builders and warhead designers who create, to the operations personnel and maintainers who make it fly, the ICBM program is truly a team effort.

The patch for Glory Trip 176/177 playfully states, "Make my shot a double." This dual launch was scheduled for September 12, 2001, but was cancelled due to the September 11 attacks on New York City and the Pentagon. It was eventually rescheduled for October 2001. Frequent Follow-on Test and Evaluation launches continually validate the training of missile combat crewmembers, as well as the reliability of the Minuteman III weapon system. (Joseph C. Iungerman.)

Six

Archaeology of the Cold War

The archaeological remnants of the various missile systems and space projects are still visible around Vandenberg. Some areas have been repurposed to support space launch missions, while others have been left to the effects of the ocean's salt air and cool winds

The base civil engineer squadron and the Aqualliers—Vandenberg's scuba diving club—retrieved the anchor of the USS *Chauncey* in 1973. As a memorial, the anchor and a plaque were placed on a slab overlooking Point Pednerales. Due to deterioration caused by the coastal climate, the anchor was moved to the Lompoc Valley Historical Society for public display. (Page Family, CA Chapter.)

Looking eerily calm on this sunny day, the Devil's Jaw awaits its next victim. The rocky outcrop in the distance is named Woodbury Rock for its prey during the Honda Point disaster. The resulting Court of Inquiry stated that "although [then current] follow-the-leader doctrine had been naval policy in matters relating to proper navigation – it must be delineated by common sense." (Page Family, CA Chapter.)

The remnants of SLC-1E remain abandoned as a forgotten memorial to the nation's space photoreconnaissance effort. There are no plans to restore the site, though ideas for a Thor National Historic District—encompassing the co-located SLC-1, SLC-2, and SLC-10 complexes—have been discussed. (Page Family, CA Chapter.)

Launch Emplacement-8 (LE-8) was used for RAF Thor Combat Training Launches (CTLs). After RAF operations ceased, the LE-8 hardware was stripped for other Thor-related projects at Vandenberg and Johnston Island. The 2000 television movie *Rocket's Red Glare* was filmed at Vandenberg and in the nearby communities of Los Alamos and Lompoc, with LE-8 standing in as the launch pad for the hero's homebuilt rocket. (Page Family, CA Chapter.)

This Titan I—serial number 60-3698—lies bisected inside the perimeter fence of 395C. "Charlie Site," as it is otherwise known, has not launched a missile since June 1976, but remains intact. Other Titan sites on base were cannibalized to outfit operational Titan silos or render them "demilitarized" and unable to launch missiles. These sites are unaffected by arms treaties stipulations and—unlike Minuteman and Peacekeeper facilities—they were not imploded. (Page Family, CA Chapter.)

Echoes of the past are seen in this present-day photograph of 395A. This corrugated aluminum tunnel shows five decades of wear and tear. The final launch from 395A took place on March 5, 1965. The complex quickly fell into disrepair and was abandoned in the subsequent decades, but is now used as a training complex for Vandenberg security forces. (Jon Haeber.)

Vandenberg's Heritage Park honors the World War II and Korean War veterans of Camp Cooke. On September 1, 2000, a memorial for veterans of the Korean War's 40th Infantry Division was dedicated on the 50th anniversary of the war. The orientation of the diamond design looks toward an oriental lantern, along the 295-degree azimuth, 5,792 miles from the Land of the Morning Calm. (Page Family, CA Chapter.)

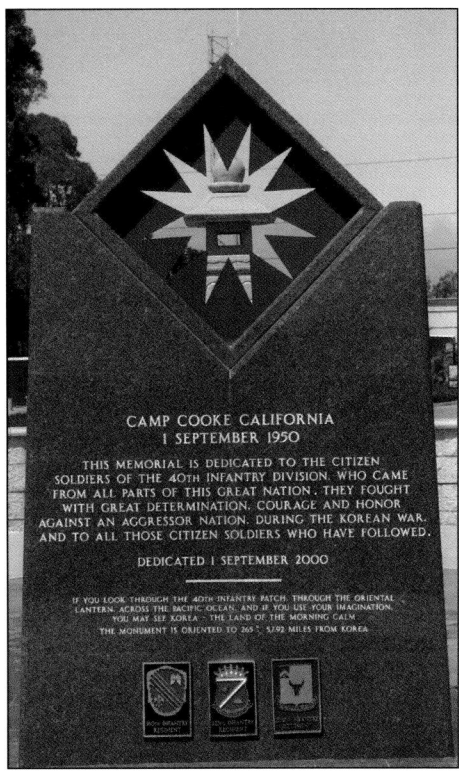

This M-47 Patton tank remains on static display at Vandenberg's Heritage Park. Memorial markers for the 5th, 6th, and 11th Armored Divisions are placed around the display, recognizing Camp Cooke's contributions in training these divisions and over 400 other separate and distinct military units during World War II and the Korean War. (Page Family, CA Chapter.)

In this photograph, a controlled explosion destroys unexploded ordnance (UXO) in North Vandenberg. Since the days of Camp Cooke, UXO has been a hazard in portions of north and south Vandenberg. When contractor crews discover UXO, one method of removal is by detonation.

The view from Tranquillion Peak offers a grand look across Sudden Ranch toward Jalama Beach and the Channel Islands. The military's interest in obtaining Robert Sudden's property began in 1956, but eased back until the MOL program hit its full stride in the mid-1960s. These lands remain undeveloped as a safety barrier against rocket explosions and urban encroachment. (Page Family, CA Chapter.)

This northward view of 13th Street shows the eroded embankments that were carved for the space shuttle's passage to South Vandenberg. The electrical poles still tower over the road, in yet another artifact of the shuttle's planned passage through Vandenberg. Similar embankments can be found along the tow road near Surf Beach. (Page Family, CA Chapter.)

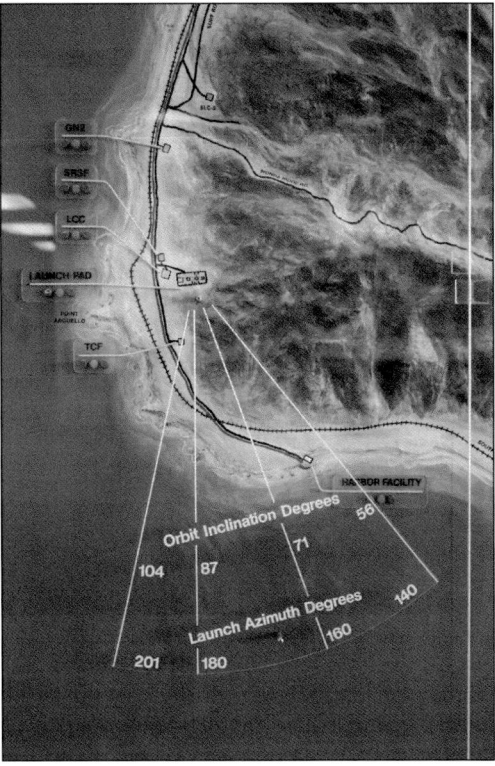

The shuttle complex, planning offices, and even a large hall for press conferences still stand at Vandenberg. Building No. 8500 contains a large wall-mounted map of Vandenberg, with status lights at each of the shuttle's planned stops through North and South Vandenberg. Note that the map included a translation overlay of the launch azimuth to orbital inclination, showing SLC-6's polar orbit range from a 56-degree to 104-degree inclination. (Page Family, CA Chapter.)

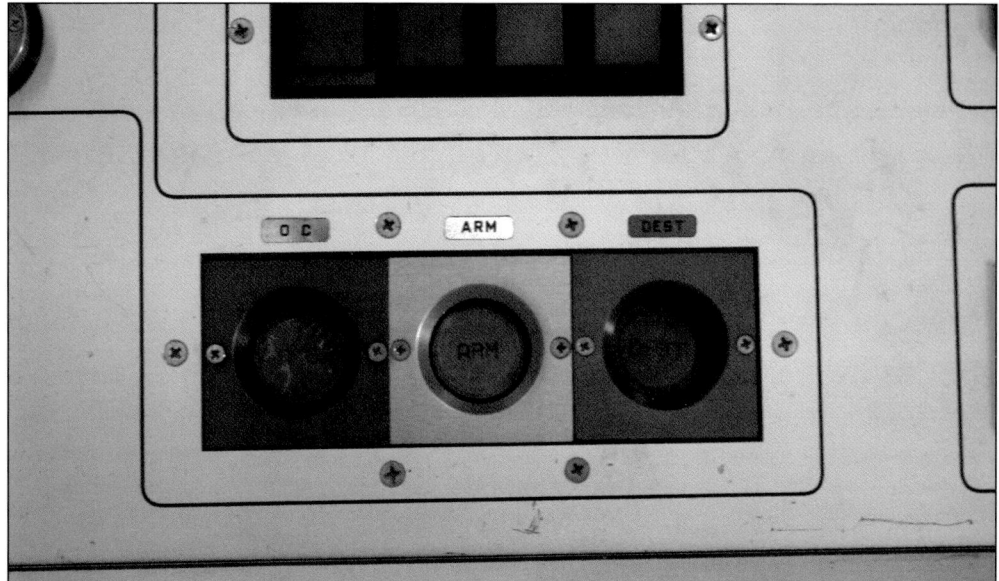

This close-up of the Mission Flight Control Officer (MFCO) console from the Western Range Operations Control Center shows the "arm" and "destruct" buttons. As a safety precaution, an MFCO monitors all launches from the Western Range—prepared to destroy the rocket if it violates any preestablished safety limits. This console is now on display at the Space and Missile Heritage Center.

At SLC-4E, the last Titan IV rocket (B-26) waits patiently for its launch on October 19, 2005. This last launch brought an end to the Titan era at Vandenberg. Two hundred launches of Titan variants took place at Vandenberg between 1961 and 2005. This mobile service tower was destroyed on August 2, 2011, to make way for SpaceX Falcon heavy booster facilities. (Lockheed Martin Corporation.)

Encased in plastic at SLC-10, this chipped floor tile is the last remaining piece of evidence of the 10th Aerospace Defense Group's work at Vandenberg. During its heyday, the 10th ADG controlled all aspects of the Program 437 anti-satellite system at Vandenberg and Johnston Island. After Program 437 ended, the 10th ADG was downgraded to a squadron and continued to operate Thor boosters for the Defense Meteorological Support Program until 1980.

The Thor IRBM's legacy lives on at SLC-2, with the Delta space launch vehicle. Many of the original Thor buildings still exist at SLC-2 alongside the modernized mobile service towers required for the larger Delta vehicles. As of 2014, there are still a handful of Delta boosters in inventory, though the program is nearing its final days.

This photograph of Atlas 27E, taken on June 7, 1961, shows the distinctive coffin launcher of the Atlas-F ICBM variant. In 2013, the 576F coffin launcher was demolished by contractor crews. While the abandoned sites around Vandenberg maintain archaeological relevance, a lack of facility upkeep has created numerous dangerous locations.

These are the remains of the Titan missile Operational Suitability Test Facility silo, near complex 395A. Chunks of rebar and concrete can still be seen surrounding the site, which is overgrown with coastal flora. Water has filled up most of the silo, and a thin layer of green algae sits on top. (Jon Haeber.)

Once an Atlas-F ICBM silo, launch complex 576E hosted Orbital Sciences' Taurus space launch vehicle from the late 1990s through the present day. Although the last Taurus launch was in 2011, and the complex looks abandoned, only two weeks are needed to get the site ready for another launch. In front of the clamshell tent to the right is the launch platform for the Taurus rocket.

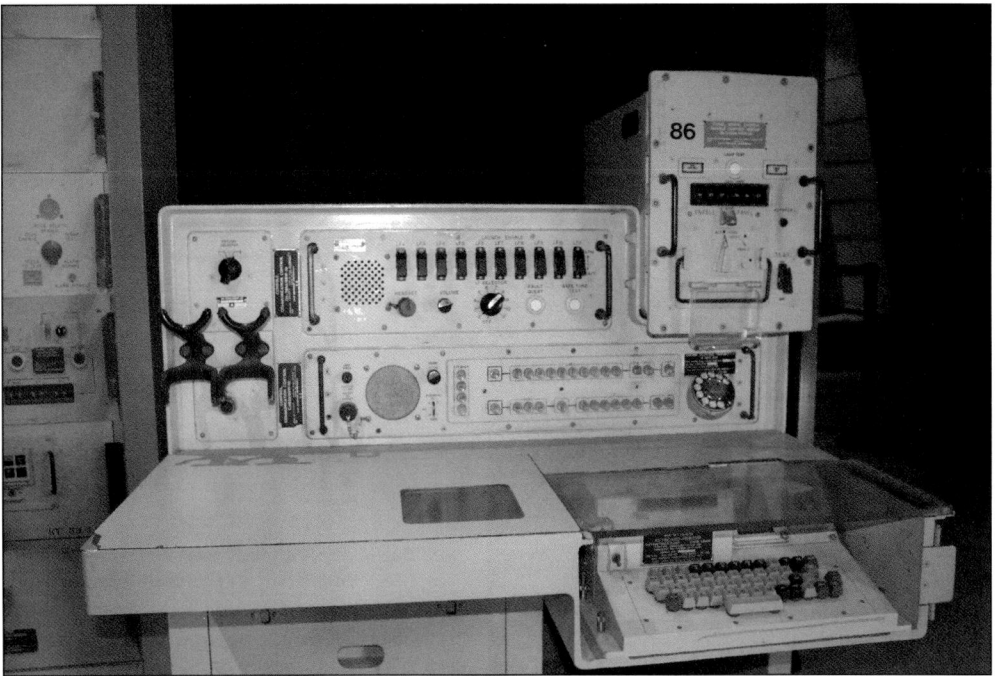

This Minuteman ICBM Deputy Missile Combat Crew Commander's console looks deceptively simple, but has the power to launch 50 missiles directly. Its rotary dial phone and clear Lucite buttons seem antiquated to today's missileers, but the function of the equipment does not vary greatly from the command and control equipment that is now in use under the plains of the Midwest.

A lone gantry at complex 576A-3 remains as visible proof of the Atlas ICBM program's home at Vandenberg. During Soviet Premier Nikita Khrushchev's visit to California in 1959, Atlas-Ds were poised in their gantries. According to an NPR interview of Sen. Jim Webb "As the train . . . entered the base's property, Khrushchev famously folded his arms and turned his back on the facility, staring out into the Pacific Ocean until his railroad car was again on civilian soil." (Page Family, CA Chapter.)

Seven

VANDENBERG SPACE AND MISSILE HERITAGE CENTER AT SLC-10

Described on the National Register of Historic Places as "the best surviving example of a launch complex built... at the beginning of the American effort to explore space," SLC-10 is the historical nexus of Vandenberg. Originally built in 1958 to launch the Thor IRBM, SLC-10 has seen space systems across a wide swath of Air Force missions, including IRBM, anti-satellite weapons, and meteorological satellites.

The complex was built by the Douglas Aircraft Company to support Thor IRBM combat training launches. Initially designated complex 75-2, construction lasted from January 1958 to October 1958, and it was accepted by the Air Force soon after. As originally designed, the SLC-10 complex consisted of three launch pads, and all three were decommissioned and stripped after the Thor IRBM program launches were discontinued in June 1962. In 1964, two launch pads (designated SLC-10E and SLC-10W) were reactivated, but launches were restricted to the western pad, closest to the ocean, while the eastern pad was used strictly for training. The last launch from SLC-10E was on March 19, 1962, and it was decommissioned and stripped shortly thereafter. The last launch from SLC-10W was on July 14, 1980, and it was then decommissioned and kept at caretaker status.

Both pads at SLC-10 remained untouched between 1980 and 1985. The next year, SLC-10 became a National Historic Landmark under the National Park Service's Man in Space program. The site was restored and converted into the Space and Missile Heritage Center.

Today, the SLC-10 Space and Missile Heritage Center includes hardware from a variety of missile and space systems, photographs and artifacts from the Corona program, and other displays relating to the space launch missions at the Western Range. Other artifacts, such as a Small ICBM casing, are currently in storage, awaiting future display.

Aside from the educational aspects of SLC-10, the location has also been scouted by Hollywood filmmakers. It was used as the prime filming location for the movie *Rocket's Red Glare*. The site is also a popular gathering location for community recreational groups, military retirements, and unit barbeques and get-togethers.

Johnston Island's Launch Emplacement 1 (LE-1) was Program 437's primary launch location until it was shut down in 1975. After the Project Emily on-alert missiles were returned to the United States, a number were reused for Program 437—American's first anti-satellite program.

These images show a Program 437 Thor being loaded with a W49 warhead on Johnston Island in 1962. The island had the dubious honor of being a nuclear test site during Operation Fishbowl in 1962. The Bluegill test was attempted three times, with the second attempt (Bluegill Prime) being destroyed on the pad by the range safety officer. This spread plutonium around Johnston Island, requiring three months of decontamination and cleanup.

The 29th and final DMSP launch at SLC-10W took place on July 15, 1980. Weather satellite technology is widespread today, but DMSP was shrouded in secrecy for almost two decades when it was first developed. As a covert satellite program within the NRO, DMSP led the way for Corona, Gambit, and Hexagon satellites in photographing cloud-free areas over the Soviet Union.

Standing in as a representative of the SLC's original resident, this Thor IRBM model is the first object seen upon walking inside the Heritage Center. Photographs of Project Emily deployments and RAF combat training launches document the rise of the Thor program.

The main museum building houses a full Atlas ICBM launch control console, as seen here. Originally used at the ABRES site, this console shows visitors the level of technology available in the late 1950s and early 1960s. The console's outdated features include rotary dial telephones and built-in ashtrays. (Page Family, CA Chapter.)

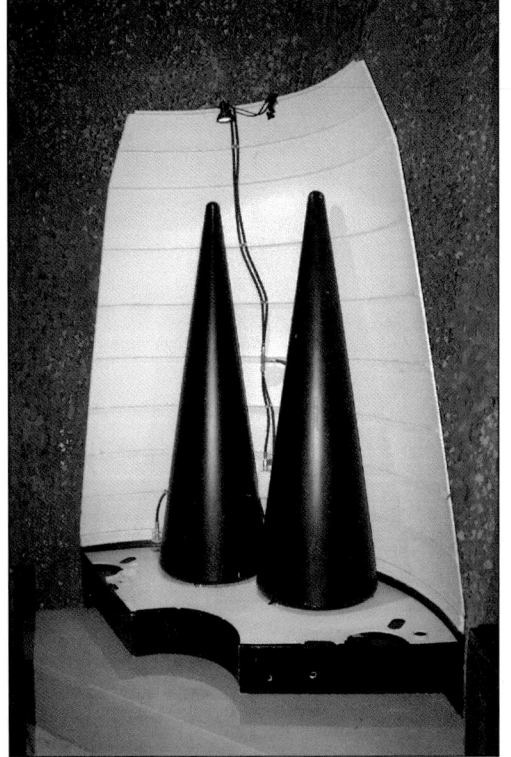

This partial cutaway model of an LGM-118A Peacekeeper shroud shows two Mark-21 reentry vehicles. The Peacekeeper missile was a critical piece of the Reagan administration's Strategic Modernization Program in the 1980s. Its range, throw weight, and accuracy bested many Soviet systems of the time. Its retirement in 2005, after 19 years on alert, left the US ICBM force with only the Minuteman III in its inventory. (Page Family, CA Chapter.)

This mock-up of an Agena upper stage is being "worked on" by two manikins in RFHCO (Rocket Fuel Handler's Coverall Outfits) suits. The declassification of the Corona program in 1995 allowed for the telling of the full story of the Thor/Agena space launch booster in the early days of the Cold War. The museum's collection features never-before-seen photographs from the early days of Corona. (Page Family, CA Chapter.)

This Mark 11 Minuteman II reentry vehicle training aid is housed in the museum's main building. The third version in the Minuteman family, this missile began development in 1965 and replaced the range-limited A- and B-variants. The first launch of a Minuteman II from Vandenberg took place on August 18, 1965, under the code name "Rebel Ranger." (Page Family, CA Chapter.)

For a missileer, this control configuration signifies a really bad day at work. Contrary to popular belief, there is no "red button" to launch a Minuteman ICBM. A simple key and knob (at left) are used. The launch key is inserted, and then rotated with three other cooperative launch switches, to initiate the user's launch vote. The same actions must then be mirrored by another launch crew to prevent an inadvertent launch. (Page Family, CA Chapter.)

The angular SLC-10W environmental shelter is located behind the heritage center's administration building. The complex is sprawling, with one building housing missile artifacts and another celebrating the space launch activities at Vandenberg. A third building, the SLC-10E and LE-8 blockhouse, houses a complete set of Thor technical data. (Page Family, CA Chapter.)

The SLC-10W environmental shelter contains a restored Thor missile in its pre-launch storage configuration. This missile was originally kept at on-alert status in the United Kingdom during Project Emily. After the IRBMs were removed from England, they were converted to space launch boosters. This particular missile survived and was put in storage at Norton Air Force Base. It was transported to Vandenberg in 1995. (Page Family, CA Chapter.)

Here, museum director Jay Prichard (center, facing camera) discusses SLC-10's history with visitors. Prichard has been involved in SLC-10's museum operations since the early 1990s. His knowledge of early liquid-fueled rockets and industrial processes has been of use during his appearances on the History Channel, and in his briefing members of the Department of Defense. (Page Family, CA Chapter.)

Museum director Jay Prichard's Ural motorcycle with sidecar, nicknamed "Yuri," sits outside SLC-10's administrative building. The inclusion of the motorcycle into the dialogue of the museum's historical narrative is incidental, but offers crucial context for younger generations in a post–Cold War world. (Page Family, CA Chapter.)

The rust-encrusted launch shelter of SLC-10E stands virtually empty, save for the remnants of historical artifacts and owl pellets. From 1959 to 1962, the pad was used for six RAF combat training launches of the Thor IRBM. The east pad later served as a crew training facility for Program 437, the nuclear-tipped anti-satellite program based at Johnston Island. (Page Family, CA Chapter.)

The "big daddy" of ICBM reentry vehicles, the LGM-25C Titan II's AVCO Mark 6 reentry vehicle had a yield of nine megatons—roughly equivalent to 600 times the power of the bomb dropped on Hiroshima. A thorough inspection by the National Nuclear Security Agency (NNSA) allowed for the Mark 6 to remain on display in a demilitarized status, with no explosives or nuclear material present. (Page Family, CA Chapter.)

The remains of this CIM-10A BOMARC anti-aircraft missile greet visitors entering the SLC-10 complex. Designed as a nuclear-tipped surface-to-air missile for the defense of North America, a diminished reliance on slower bomber aircraft and heavier emphasis on ICBMs relegated BOMARC to other roles soon after its introduction. Vandenberg launched 56 A-variants and 31 B-variants between 1966 and 1982, as flying targets for other surface-to-air and air-to-air missile systems.

The west pad at SLC-10 provides a unique location for a barbeque and unit gathering for the Unified Space Vault. The shelter has seen its share of gatherings, ranging from a birthday party for Gen. Bernard Schriever to military retirements. SLC-10 remains one of the few places on Vandenberg that allows "up close and personal" viewing of missile hardware. The site's legacy is best experienced by walking around. (Page Family, CA Chapter.)

The SLC-10 parking lot is filled with cars from the Ferrari Club of America in this photograph from a 2014 visit. The launch complex hosts visits from schools, clubs, and individuals all throughout the year. Anyone with access to Vandenberg may visit the site during its weekday hours, while interested parties without access to the base can arrange a visit by contacting the base's Public Affairs Office.

This "Death Wears Bunny Slippers" morale patch shows the macabre sense of humor common to missileers. The seriousness of alert responsibilities is not lost on these young men and women. However, the opportunity to wear morale patches allows missileers to display pride in their work, their weapon system, and their nation's defense. And yes, some missileers do wear bunny slippers while on alert. (Joseph C. Iungerman.)

The author, pictured here as a young second lieutenant in May 2001, stands next to a model of a Minuteman III at SLC-10. After an assignment as a Minuteman III missile combat crewmember at Minot Air Force Base in North Dakota, he performed various space-related jobs until arriving back at Vandenberg over a decade later. (Page Family, CA Chapter.)

Driving through Vandenberg's main gate, visitors approach the "Missile V"—a forked road leading to the housing complex and operations side of base. At this junction, a greeting sign clearly states "Welcome to Space Country." With the diligence and derring-do required in the early days of the Cold War, the United States created the world's premier operational space and missile launch program at Vandenberg. That legacy continues today. (Page Family, CA Chapter.)

BIBLIOGRAPHY

Arnold, David C. *Spying From Space: Constructing America's Satellite Command and Control Systems.* College Station, TX: Texas A&M University Press, 2005.

Berger, Carl. *History of the 1st Strategic Aerospace Division and Vandenberg Air Force Base 1957–1961.* Vandenberg AFB, CA: 1STRAD History Office.

Del Papa, Michael. *From Snark to Peacekeeper: A Pictorial History of Strategic Air Command Missiles.* Omaha, NE: Office of the Historian, Strategic Air Command, 1990.

Geiger, Jeffrey. *From Tanks to Missiles: Vandenberg Air Force Base and the 30th Space Wing from Camp Cooke to the Present.* Vandenberg AFB, CA: 30th Space Wing History Office, 1995.

Gibson, James N. *Nuclear Weapons of the United States: An Illustrated History.* Atglen, PA: Schiffer Publishing Ltd., 1996.

Heefner, Gretchen. *The Missile Next Door: The Minuteman in the American Heartland.* Boston, MA: Harvard University Press, 2012.

Lonnquest, John, and David Winkler. *To Defend and Deter: The Legacy of the United States Cold War Missile Program.* Washington, DC: Department of Defense Legacy Resource Management Program, 1996.

Narducci, Henry. *Strategic Air Command and the Alert Program: A Brief History.* Omaha, NE: Office of the Historian, Strategic Air Command, 1988.

Neal, Roy. *Ace in the Hole: The Story of the Minuteman Missile.* New York, NY: Doubleday Press, 1962.

Palmer, Kevin. *Central Coast Continuum – From Ranchos to Rockets.* Santa Maria, CA: BTG Inc., 1999.

Peebles, Curtis. *The CORONA Project: America's First Spy Satellites.* Annapolis, MD: Naval Institute Press, 1997.

Polmar, Norman, and Robert S. Norris. *The U.S. Nuclear Arsenal: A History of Weapons and Delivery Systems since 1945.* Annapolis, MD: Naval Institute Press, 2009.

Spires, David. *On Alert: An Operational History Of The United States Air Force Intercontinental Ballistic Missile Program, 1945–2011.* Colorado Springs, CO: Air Force Space Command History Office, 2012.

Vandenberg AFB Launch Summary 1957–2010. Vandenberg AFB, CA: 30th Space Wing History Office, 2010.

Waltrop, David. *An Underwater Ice Station Zebra: Recovering a Secret Spy Capsule from 16,400 feet Below the Pacific Ocean.* Langley, VA: Central Intelligence Agency, 2012.

INDEX

Agena, 43, 48, 53, 54, 86, 117
Argon, 10, 54
Atlas, 9, 10, 29–33, 35–37, 43, 46, 53, 82, 83, 86, 110–112, 116, 127
Boathouse, 14, 71, 94
BOMARC, 79, 121
Camp Cooke, 8, 11, 19–25, 105, 106
Corona, 2, 10, 43, 47–58, 113, 115, 117, 127
Curtain Raiser, 29, 40, 41, 80
Delta, 42, 64, 83, 109
Delta IV, 64, 83
Discoverer, 48, 52, 53, 55
Gambit, 10, 43, 47, 53–56, 58, 60–62, 86, 115
GPS, 82
Hexagon, 10, 47, 54–59, 62, 70, 86, 115
Honda Canyon fire, 66–68
Honda Point, 7, 11, 13, 17, 102
Honda Ridge, 12, 86
Kennedy, John F., 29, 34–37, 52, 92
Lanyard, 10, 47, 54
Manned Orbiting Laboratory, 44, 69, 106
Marshallia Ranch, 15, 45
Mathison, Col. Charles "Moose," 52, 53
Minuteman, 10, 29, 32, 37–42, 65, 76, 78, 80, 85, 87, 88, 93, 100, 104, 111, 116–118, 123, 127
Missile combat crewmembers, 10, 35, 78, 80, 81, 87, 100, 111, 123
National Imagery Interpretability Rating Scale (NIIRS), 50
National Reconnaissance Office, 10, 47–64, 70, 115
Olympic Arena, 29, 79, 80, 81, 84, 85
Peacekeeper, 65, 76–78, 80, 87, 104, 116, 127
Point Pedernales, 11, 16, 17
Quill, 10, 47, 54,
Rail Garrison, 77, 78, 87
SLC-1, 2, 49, 103
SLC-2, 49, 103, 109
SLC-3, 43, 49, 81, 82
SLC-4, 54, 58, 86, 108
SLC-6, 44, 64, 65, 69–74, 107
SLC-10, 31, 103, 109, 113–124,127
Soviet Union, 10, 38, 39, 47, 50–53, 112, 115, 116

Space and Missile Heritage Center, 54, 108, 113–124, 127
Space shuttle, 14, 44, 58, 65, 69–75
Teal Ruby, 75
Thrust Augmented Thor, 49
Thorad, 48, 49
Titan I, 10, 32, 33, 45, 104
Titan II, 29, 41, 42, 44, 45, 65, 99, 121
Titan III, 44, 45, 54, 86
Titan IV, 45, 63, 83, 86, 108, 127
Thor, 2, 9, 10, 28, 29, 31, 42, 43, 49, 54, 83, 103, 109, 113–115, 117–120, 127
Vandenberg, Hoyt S., 9, 26, 27

About the Vandenberg Space and Missile Heritage Center

Vandenberg's Space and Missile Heritage Center, located at SLC-10, preserves and displays artifacts and memorabilia that interpret the evolution of missile and space lift activity at Vandenberg—from the beginning of the Cold War through current non-classified developments in military, commercial, and scientific space endeavors.

The initial display area is made up of two exhibits, "Chronology of the Cold War," and "Evolution of Technology." The exhibits incorporate a combination of launch complex models, launch consoles, rocket engines, reentry vehicles, audiovisual and computer displays, and hands-on interaction. The center will evolve in stages from these initial exhibit areas as the restoration of additional facilities are completed.

Exhibits at SLC-10 include:

Photographs and hardware from the CORONA program

Training hardware for missile maintenance crews

Launch control center consoles from Minuteman

Displays showcasing the various designs of missile reentry vehicles

A full-size training replica of the Peacekeeper Mark 21 reentry vehicle

A full Atlas ICBM launch console from the 576th ABRES complex

A restored Thor IRBM in launch configuration status

A 1/20th scale model of SLC-4W Titan IV Launch Gantry

Memorabilia from Brig. Gen. William "Bill" King

The center is located at Space Launch Complex 10—Vandenberg's only National Historic Landmark—and is open for regularly scheduled tours through the public affairs office, at 805-606-3595. Persons with normal base access may contact the center directly at 805-605-8300.

DISCOVER THOUSANDS OF LOCAL HISTORY BOOKS FEATURING MILLIONS OF VINTAGE IMAGES

Arcadia Publishing, the leading local history publisher in the United States, is committed to making history accessible and meaningful through publishing books that celebrate and preserve the heritage of America's people and places.

Find more books like this at
www.arcadiapublishing.com

Search for your hometown history, your old stomping grounds, and even your favorite sports team.

Consistent with our mission to preserve history on a local level, this book was printed in South Carolina on American-made paper and manufactured entirely in the United States. Products carrying the accredited Forest Stewardship Council (FSC) label are printed on 100 percent FSC-certified paper.

MADE IN THE USA